Captain Carteret and the Voyage of the Swallow

H.G. Mowat

This book is dedicated to the memory of
Captain H.G. Mowat
and to Jeanne, Sheila, Robert & Penny

© 2011 H.G. Mowat. All rights reserved
ISBN 978-1-4709-0079-3

Contents

Chapter I 3
Chapter II 13
Chapter III 26
Chapter IV 41
Chapter V 58
Chapter VI 72
Chapter VII 81
Chapter VIII 94
Chapter IX 108
Chapter X 116
Chapter XI 131
Chapter XII 142
Chapter XIII 159
Chapter XIV 175
Chapter XV 185
Chapter XVI 193
Illustrations 202
References 207
Index 208

Chapter I

Lieutenant Philip Carteret, recently discharged from His Britannic Majesty's frigate *Dolphin* after a voyage of exploration under Commodore the Hon. John Byron and at this time on half pay, must surely have been pleased to receive a communication from the Admiralty on July 3rd 1766, requesting and requiring him to make his way to Chatham where the sloop *Swallow* was being fitted out ready for sea.

Britain at this time was in the midst of a period of peace with her old enemies France and Spain, the Peace Treaty of Fontainbleau having been signed only a year previously. Thus, with ships laid up and numerous officers on the beach urgently seeking employment, the appointment would have been most welcome to Carteret although it would remove him from the bosom of his family barely six weeks after his return from a two year voyage to the far side of the world. However, the communication, when it reached his home in St Malo was doubly welcome since it contained his appointment as Commander of the sloop *Swallow* and an order to prepare her for a voyage to the Pacific in search of the great southern continent thought to exist there.

Carteret, a member of a leading Jersey family with many years of association with the Navy, could count among his ancestors Sir George de Carteret, erstwhile treasurer of the Navy in Pepys's time. Therefore it is not surprising that in October of 1751 at the age of fourteen he went off to join his first ship, the *Salisbury,* commanded by the Hon. George Edgecumbe. He was already on her books, his father, Charles de Carteret having entered his name twelve months previously, a common practice in order to secure early seniority but one much frowned upon by their Lordships. He was rated on the *Salisbury* as an officer's servant but remained only three months joining the *Monmouth* as a volunteer early the following year. November 1751 finds him on board the *St Albans* where her Captain the Hon. John Byron, sensing the boy's potential, took him to his next command the *Augusta*, thence the *Vanguard* from 1753 to 1757. During his time on the *Vanguard* he passed for lieutenant, the date being August 1755, and later saw action in the English Channel and Mediterranean under Captain Mark Millbanke in the *Guernsey*.

In 1762 when Byron was in command of the *Dolphin*, he chose Carteret to be first lieutenant on the *Tamar*, the second ship on a voyage of exploration to the Pacific; during the voyage he promoted him first lieutenant on the *Dolphin*. It was a good choice: Carteret was a competent seaman and navigator, the forthcoming voyage on the *Swallow* proved it, and his perseverance against all odds reveals a strong character and remarkable sense of duty; he was by all accounts considerate to his men who repaid him with their unstinting loyalty. This came out strongly during the subsequent voyage. His star is in its ascendancy: promotion at twenty-eight even to a sixth rate ship is a smile of fortune; and with the influence of Byron, now elevated to the peerage, he can expect if he is not carried off by a cannon ball or the yellow jack, a steady rise to flag rank in the forthcoming years. There are two portraits of him, no date to either, although one may be when he was Rear-Admiral, urbane, portly and prosperous. The other, executed at an earlier age, is little more than a silhouette, but one which never-the-less gives the impression of a determined and dogged personality. It was against his nature ever to accept second best and this on occasion put him at odds with the Admiralty.

A sailor's first command is often a special one regarded with particular affection, its looks, faults and blemishes accepted with a degree of tolerance. However, on July 5th, when Carteret first set foot on the *Swallow*, he would have had mixed feelings as it was soon apparent to him that her needs were many and must be satisfied before she would be fit for a long voyage of exploration in distant waters. Sloops like the *Swallow* came in different sizes and rigs, and at best were the handmaidens of the Navy, only suitable for minor roles such as coastal defence, convoying merchant ships, defending them against corsairs, pirates and privateers or any enemy ship of comparable size and armament. They could also be adapted to the more peaceful purposes of transport, survey duties and exploration.

But now it was time to give his command a thorough inspection, an appraisal of her requirements with a view to fitting her out as speedily as possible. His instructions were clear about this in order to reach the Pacific in time for the southern summer. He had definite misgivings about her since although over twenty years old, she had never been to sea, the role of an impress ship having been her lot, permanently moored in the dull reaches of the River Medway, a virtual prison hulk. Her plans held in the Archives of the National Maritime Museum tell us that she was a 'Falcon' class sloop of twelve guns built at Rotherhythe in 1745. Her measurements are given in the draughtsman's own words as follows:-

Length on the Range of the Deck	91ft 0ins
By the keel for tonnage	74ft 9ins
Breadth Extream	26ft 0ins
Height between Decks	5ft 0ins
Burthen in Tunns	269
Draught -Afore	10 ft 7ins
-Abaft	11ft 0ins

Further details on the plan state "To Carry 6 pounders 12 No", "Swivel Guns 14", "Men 110" and 32 oars.

In fact the plans, if Carteret ever saw them, differed from the ship that he took command of that day early in July 1766. His first sight of her before he set foot on her deck told him that although laid down as a brig, a mizen mast had been added complete with topsail and crossjack yards, so she was in fact a full-rigged ship.[1] Furthermore, her forecastle and poop appeared to have been extended, probably to give more shelter on deck from the weather as required in her duties as 'impress' ship. A count of the number of gun ports revealed fourteen which made her a fourteen gun sloop and Carteret always referred to her as such. Some work on her had already been carried out on the orders of the Admiralty to make her more seaworthy including the construction of bulkheads on the after end of the forecastle and beneath the fore end of the poop. Also the height of her masts had been reduced, the fore and main masts by twenty-nine and eleven inches respectively and the bowsprit by twelve inches and the jibboom by eight. The construction of the bulkheads was of great benefit, one might say a godsend and in the event may well have saved her from foundering months later off the coast of Chile; but as far as the reduction of the length of the spars is concerned it did nothing for her sailing qualities, in fact it may have impaired them.

There were other apparent departures from the original plans: the sail room had been taken over for other duties, possibly for accommodation for a warrant officer; the spirit room was inadequate for a crew numbering the best part of a hundred and the capstan was badly sited. These needed adjusting immediately.

As yet no officers had been appointed to the *Swallow* with whom Carteret might have discussed her needs but the ship's carpenter was available: he had been on the *Swallow's* muster for twenty years, John Renshaw by name, and between the two of them a list of requirements was soon compiled, a modest one in all fairness considering the ship's commitments but one which

---

[1] With the mizzen added she became in the Royal Navy a 'Ship Sloop'.

was pared down by the Admiralty in due course.

The first request for alteration was the capstan to be resited on the quarter-deck, the only place where there would be sufficient space for the important evolutions such as weighing anchor, raising topgallant and topmasts or hoisting boats aboard, in fact any job where additional purchase was needed. The next item concerned the need for a ladder or companionway from under the poop to the lower or 'tween deck for use in bad weather when the after bulkhead doors were closed. Thirdly, the lack of a sailroom and the size of the spirit room had to be addressed and Carteret suggested that the former be constructed in the 'eyes' of the ship while the spirit room be built right aft on the after platform against the bread room. He also urged that the channels be widened as the existing ones gave too little spread to the shrouds which chafed on the bulwark rail. Furthermore he requested an awning to be fitted over the poop.

The Admiralty agreed to these requests except the awning which they considered not quite the thing to have over a quarter-deck; they also quibbled about the capstan, but Carteret won the day and it was duly moved. Another important consideration and source of disappointment to him were the boats. The importance of good boats for a ship cannot be overstressed. Transporting personnel to and from the shore was but one of their duties: they were in constant demand for ferrying stores, water and equipment to the ship while other tasks included rescue, sounding, surveying, towing anything from targets for gunnery practice to the ship herself when caught in stays or in calms to and from an anchorage or harbour. For these purposes the *Swallow* was supplied with a cutter, a clinker-built boat of about twenty-four feet pulling eight oars, and a long-boat described by Carteret as "a clumsy four-oared craft" which he didn't think very highly of. To compensate for the long-boat's shortcomings he made a request for a jolly-boat or skiff, a six-oared clinker built craft which could be usefully employed for most jobs and light enough to be easily hoisted in and out. The cutter and long-boat would be stowed on deck fore and aft between the main-mast and the fore-hatch, but in the tropics they would be towed astern when possible in order to keep the seams tight. Unfortunately the Admiralty refused his request for the jolly-boat.

Meanwhile, Carteret was trying to gather together a crew for the *Swallow*, no easy matter in spite of the offer of two months advance of pay. A voyage of exploration was an uncertain project to embark on: the risks were high, death by scurvy being one of them, to say nothing of the hazards of reef and storm. A voyage of indeterminate length into unknown waters was not to be taken lightly and many seamen who had already completed one voyage were unwilling to do another. Furthermore the double pay received by the crew on Byron's voyage was not forthcoming this time. Meanwhile time was passing and the Admiralty were impatient to get the ship to sea.

On the 12th July, Erasmus Gower joined the *Swallow*. Carteret knew him well having sailed with him on the *Dolphin* when Gower was Master's mate but now promoted to lieutenant. He was in his early twenties and was to prove a great asset on the forthcoming voyage. A week later on the 18th the Master, Alexander Simpson joined. He was a Scot from Angus and had also been with Byron. Midshipman Pitcairn, 19 years old from Edinburgh, came the same day, followed by Midshipman William Rowe, also 19, who hailed from Quethiok in Cornwall. There were other officers whom the *Swallow* was short of; no purser nor surgeon as yet, but in time the warrant officers joined, five in number, namely the gunner, bosun, carpenter and 2 Master's mates. This, together with the purser and surgeon, 68 seamen and boys, plus a corporal and 10 marines, would bring the *Swallow's* complement to a total of 90 souls.

Gradually Carteret collected a crew together. Among those who joined, some deserted before long. However, eventually the following were assembled:-

Lieutenant	1
Master	1
Master's mates	2
Midshipmen	2
Surgeon	1
Purser	1
Gunner	1
Carpenter	1
Boatswain	1
Marine Corporal	1
Marines	10
Seamen and Boys	68
Total	90

From the total of 68 seamen and boys would be drawn bosun's mates, officer's servants, cooks, also tradesmen required to keep the ship running, coopers, sailmakers and blacksmiths. Later a 'Watch Bill' would be devised allotting each man a duty, bosun's mates, topmen, quartermasters, cooks, powder monkeys, officers' servants and finally the lowest of them all, the waisters, i.e. landsmen drafted in with no nautical experience. All these men had to be fed and yet, on the plans of the *Swallow*, no part of the ship was set aside for a galley. In fact the only clue to one is marked on the forecastle immediately abaft the foremast between the mooring bits, reading 'chimney funnel', and somewhere beneath, within the forecastle, immediately between the bosun's store and the carpenter's was a galley range or stove where the cooking for the whole crew was carried out. A very noticeable absence was a privy, not even the Captain had one, although there may have been a commode arrangement in the steerage for him and possibly the Officers may have had a similar arrangement somewhere. For those before the mast there were only the 'heads', triangular gratings on either side of the stem reached by clambering over the fore end of the fo'c'sle head, an uncomfortable perch even in the finest weather, but the only place for the best part of a hundred men to relieve themselves.

It is difficult to imagine where that number of men could live on board a ship about the size of a present day tug, albeit a fairly large one and at the same time fight fourteen guns and go to sea with stores and water for six months. The Captain and officers were well catered for under the circumstances, the Captain with the most palatial quarters as one would expect. He occupied the Great Cabin beneath the poop, all bright and airy with a window at each side and all the light in the world filtering through the stern windows across the transom, 10 ft x 22 ft and 7 ft headroom. For sleeping or eating he had the steerage, no longer used for that purpose now that a wheel had taken the place of the whipstaff. There were six cabins beneath the steerage and quarter-deck where the lieutenant, master, gunner, surgeon, purser and captain's clerk dwelt, each about 6 ft x 6 ft but with only 5 ft headroom, neither porthole nor ventilation but at least a place of refuge, each of his own, to retire and sleep. No bunks were needed, swinging cots being the usual means of repose from captain and officers while hammocks were the order of the day for the seamen in tiers athwartships, each man being allowed 14 inches from his neighbour on either side.

The space remaining after the ship's company had taken up their allotted berths allowed stowage of approximately 50 ft of the hold, right across the beam of the ship with a depth of 10 ft between the platform and the keelson. This would be crammed to capacity with ship's stores, to a large extent consisting of victuals for six months, barrel upon barrel of salt pork and beef, sauerkraut, cheese and as many of beer as can be conveniently stowed all in tiers eight high but no higher since beyond this, those in the lowest tier would open up and spoil, all to be stowed in such a manner to be accessible when required. Another consideration was water, a most important one and a commodity not always easy to come by in foreign parts, always rationed, never liberally, used only for cooking and drinking purposes.

No captain could afford to pass a watering place be it a river, stream or coastal creek without sending a cutter with as many empty barrels as possible available to be replenished. The barrels, each containing 36 gallons were no light weight to heave round from shore to boat, boat to ship and ship to the hold, 30 to 40 tons or thereabouts at 6 barrels per ton. They required a block stow in the hold chocked firmly on either side stowed bung up and bilge free.[2]

Further space was taken up with other items necessary to keep the ship at sea for six months; canvas, rope, blocks and tackle, powder and shot, none of it in Carteret's mind as nearly sufficient for the forthcoming voyage, in fact, because of this deficiency he was doubtful if the *Swallow* was ever intended to go beyond the Falklands.

His doubts were not unreasonable under the circumstances. The Spanish Government had been aware of the preparations for a possible voyage of exploration. Any warship sailing down the western side of the Atlantic was bound to concern them since their colonies stretched from Mexico right round the Continent of North and South America to California and they considered the islands of the Pacific Ocean, either discovered or as yet undiscovered, theirs by right. Then there were the Falkland Islands, desolate and storm-swept, with a climate that did not encourage colonisation, but nonetheless which the Spanish considered to be theirs. However, they appeared to be less concerned with a British expedition with view to a settlement, no one as yet had made a successful one, in fact the French were about to abandon theirs in the East Falklands after only a short period. What better for the Admiralty to create rumours, a smoke

---

[2] Much larger barrels might be used. 'Butts' of 108 gallons, even 'Tuns' of twice that capacity but these would be stowed in the hold permanently and when full, act as ballast and add to the ship's stability.

screen in fact, to cover their true intent by putting it about that Wallis's destination was the Falkland Islands! For good measure the Leeward Islands was also mooted as a possible destination.

Meanwhile, Carteret was being pressed to complete his preparations as quickly as possible and join Wallis at the Nore. The last days of July found the *Swallow* as ready for sea as she ever would be and whatever his misgivings about the voyage, in the space of three weeks Carteret had completed the task of gathering together a crew at the same time converting a virtual hulk of a ship into a vessel ready to proceed to sea on a voyage of discovery. He was still concerned that he did not have sufficient equipment, the forge and skiff having been refused and in the way of stores, he was also short, particularly of 'junk' for making rope, but he was told he would receive these later from the store ship *Prince Frederick*. He also requested that the *Swallow* be docked for a tide in order to have her bottom scrubbed clean as it had become foul with dirt and marine growth as a result of lying so long in the River Medway. But he was refused. This seemed unreasonable to Carteret and lack of concern by the Admiralty to comply with his requests irked him; but equally the repetition of his requests displeased their Lordships and he was told quite firmly that in their opinion the *Swallow* was perfectly fit and stored and ordered him to get her to the Nore directly and join the *Dolphin*. This he did, but before she left he was told to send all the ship's boys ashore, the voyage being deemed to dangerous for youngsters. On Saturday, 2nd August, with his crew reduced to 77 men, Carteret left his moorings at Chatham and sailed for the Nore.

Chapter II

The passage down the Medway did not go smoothly. Under the direction of a local pilot, the *Swallow* left her moorings and immediately revealed her shortcomings by missing stays, only narrowly avoiding running aground on the mud. This happened again before she reached her anchorage and anyone watching from the shore might have wondered if the pilot was drunk or the crew a bunch of unseamanlike lubbers.

Putting a full-rigged ship about in confined waters can be a tricky evolution. Eddies of wind and tide can mar it. A tidy manoeuvre, well executed, can be a measure of the ship's smartness, the critical moment being when she comes up into the eye of the wind, sails shaking and booming until, on the order "mains'l haul!," the yards come round and away she flies on the other tack. However, if all does not go well, adjustments can be made such as staying the masts slightly aft or trimming the ship further by the head by shifting the stores forward; time to attend to all this when at anchor at the Nore.

As it turned out there was time in plenty: time for Carteret to get to know his officers, gauge their capabilities and for the crew to settle in and learn the ropes. In his comfortable quarters in the Great Cabin, Carteret might have wondered what the hurry was. Local ships came and went as the *Swallow* lay swinging idly to her anchor for over a week. On the ninth day a boat came alongside with an order from the Admiralty to put himself under the command of Captain Samuel Wallis who was expected shortly at the Nore. He arrived from Deptford on 11th August in the *Dolphin*, a fine frigate, a sixth-rate of 511 tons and 24 guns, a ship which had already proved herself having completed a circumnavigation under Commodore the Hon. John Byron. She was fresh out of dock, newly coppered and stored with the best of everything for another voyage of discovery.

The arrival of a ship so well fitted out in every respect compared with his own vessel, increased Carteret's doubts about the *Swallow's* ultimate destination. Neither was Captain Wallis in any way forthcoming about it, but since he was under his orders he weighed anchor and proceeded in company with the *Dolphin* bound for Plymouth. It was now that the difference in speed between the two ships became apparent and although they kept together as far as the Downs, thereafter they parted company, the *Swallow* coming to anchor in the Plymouth Sound on Monday 18th, two days after the *Dolphin*.

Plymouth, in the days before Rennie's breakwater was built, was an open roadstead where ships could lie comfortably at anchor sheltered from the north and west. Between the Hoe and Drake's Island, the River Tamar leads up past Milbay and so on to Devonport where Carteret had high hopes of obtaining some much needed stores, particularly with regard to junk: this was to be the last port of call and the chance of getting any. But he was out of luck; no stores were forthcoming as the officer in charge of the dockyard had not received orders from the Admiralty to give him any; if he required further he would get them from the store-ship *Prince Frederick* which was to accompany them as far as the Falkland Islands. However, while in the Sound he did get some repairs done to the *Swallow's* hull: there were leaks finding a way into the lower deck which had shown up on the passage from the Nore and these were put right by caulking the seams in the strakes between wind and water.

On Thursday, 21st August, the *Dolphin* and *Swallow* in company with the *Prince Frederick* weighed anchor and set sail for Madeira. The coast of Cornwall as it receded into the distance would be the last sight of their homeland that the crew would see for the best part of two years. Some would never return, death by misadventure or scurvy would be their lot. But now the waiting was over; proceeding at the speed of the slowest ship they made their way steadily south. As Carteret wrote in his journal, nothing remarkable happened during the passage, but he noted that the *Swallow* sailed almost as well as the *Prince Frederick*. This was one of the few compliments that he paid the poor old ship, but it was a point in her favour as the *Prince Frederick* was new, a vessel of twenty guns, captured from the Spanish in the war when she was the *Viceroy*. Nonetheless, they made no great speed, the time being seventeen days between departure and landfall, an overall daily average of eighty miles from noon to noon. Thus on Sunday, 7th September, the tree-covered slopes of Mount Pica Ruevo, the Red Peak, on the Portuguese island of Madeira, hove in sight and later that day, the little fleet anchored in the roads about a mile distant from the port of Funchal.

During the next five days in this pleasant sub-tropical island, the three ships refilled their empty barrels with fresh water and took on board stocks of wine for the voyage and although suitably well supplied for the time, Carteret was concerned about other stores. It was sufficiently important for him to put pen to paper and send Wallis a letter stating his pressing need particularly for junk. Junk consists of old rope or cables cut up in lengths which are teased out by the sailors into yarns in order to make sennet or robands, or to be twisted and relaid into rope for reef points, ratlines, gaskets, even tops'l tyes, also chafing mats to prevent wear and tear on the sails where they touched the rigging, and of course oakum for caulking decks and ship's side. He explained in his letter that when in Chatham he had ordered 20 cwt but had received only 5, and as he pointed out, for want of this commodity, the spare set of sails stitched and assembled during the voyage could not be completed, thus leaving only those sails bent to the yards fit for use.

One wonders why Carteret's reasonable request met with

only a measly 5 cwt. The answer may lie with the *Dolphin's* bosun. A good bosun guarded his stores diligently, neither issuing any unless strictly necessary nor wasting so much as a rope-yarn if it could be helped and certainly never parting with any without being compelled to, since the surplus remaining at the end of the voyage was his perquisite to be sold and the proceeds pocketed, a valuable source of income indeed. As one might expect, this small amount was a disappointment to Carteret and he wrote in his Journal, "I was in a short time after, under the disagreeable (sic) necessity, to have recourse, and to cut off some of my cables, in order to have those things that were requisite to preserve my rigging."

After the disappointment over his request for stores, Carteret was soon confronted with another problem. During the stay in Madeira Roads no shore leave had been granted, perhaps for fear of desertions. This was a sad blow for the crew with two months of their pay advanced in Chatham burning holes in their pockets and the shore with all the wine and women they could desire only a mile distant. One quiet evening, it was Sunday, with only a few hands on anchor duty there were stealthy movements below decks which escaped the notice of the watch and not until early the next morning, after all hands had been called, was it found that several men were missing. When Lieutenant Gower called Carteret and acquainted him with the news that eight men had deserted, he admitted to being much disturbed as some of the ship's best hands were involved and the possibility of replacing them was remote.

Desertion was always something to be reckoned with, hence the chosen anchorage being a mile offshore; that alone should have been sufficient deterrent and with a party of marines aboard, escape should have been impossible. The Corporal and his men would have to answer for this neglect of duty in due course. But how did they get ashore was the question? Did they take a boat? Yet none were missing. A raft perhaps? The question was soon resolved. They had swum! One of the conspirators had not reached the shore being terrified by the heavy surf breaking and returned to the ship. On being questioned he replied that they had stripped naked, leaving their clothes on board, taking only their money in a handkerchief tied round their waist.

One thing was certain, the men must be recovered. Ordering the cutter to be prepared, he penned a letter to the Consul, but while he was doing so a boat came from the shore with a message that the men had been apprehended and a request for a boat to bring them back. This was done immediately.

On the face of it, this appeared to be a clear case of desertion and the guilty men as they clambered aboard were in a sorry state, naked and hang-dog. The penalty could be severe not hanging, but the cat-o'-nine tails at the grating must surely await them, and this would be the minimum which they could expect. What ensued was characteristic of Carteret's views on human relationships in the closed community of his ship. He contemplated the situation in the solitude of the Great Cabin, while Lieutenant Gower ordered all hands to muster to witness punishment. Should he make an example of these men? They deserved it without doubt, would most surely expect summary punishment and this would be the opinion of all on board. Or was it not an opportunity to show leniency? This gesture would bind the crew more firmly together and generate a spirit of loyalty strong enough to see them all through the dangers and hardships which lay ahead.

With all this in mind, he went out onto the quarter-deck. Waiting there for him to appear were Lieutenant Gower and the warrant officers; further forward on the maindeck were the marines guarding the prisoners and beyond them the rest of the crew impatient to hear what the sentence would be. But nobody was more impatient than the prisoners, as Carteret wrote in his Journal. "To my great satisfaction I immediately observed in their countenance a thorough consciousness of having behaved improperly and at the same time a readiness to undergo any punishment I should be pleased to inflict." Sensing the mood of the assembly, he decided that if it was not a case of desertion, no more than a spur of the moment escapade, an attitude of forbearance would bring its reward. But at any rate they must be made to understand that no further lapse of discipline would be tolerated. Thus, he demanded to know why they deserted the ship. "Why," he thundered, "why did they expose themselves to such risks, the danger of being eaten by sharks or the chance of drowning on a dangerous coast at such a time when their country and their ship needed them?"

The answer was simple: no one man was picked out as the leader; they all put it to him that it was the desire for one last run ashore on the eve of a long uncertain voyage during which they might live or die, to swim there for a last drink, a skinful of liquor as they put it, in order to spend the money on one last fling and then return to the ship without disturbing anyone. But, as they explained, their plans had been foiled by the damned meddling Portuguese and as a result they were discovered and everything had gone awry. They were wrong. They admitted with a wholeheartedness which convinced Carteret that they were sorry they had incurred his displeasure. Desertion was furthest from their thoughts they assured him, and they were willing to go with him wherever he should command them and would not quit the ship as long as she could swim.

In consideration of their genuine penitence and loyalty, Carteret told them that he would waive the punishment which they deserved and that from now on he expected they would give no further cause for complaint. He added that if in future he required good swimmers, he would know where to apply. He then, in his own words, "bid them lie down," as I was well assured they wanted rest. At this pronouncement a gentle whisper of satisfaction was heard from the ship's company.

All this was in complete contrast to the iron discipline generally maintained aboard ships of the Royal Navy. Carteret's lenient attitude towards the defaulters might be construed as weakness. But he held a high opinion of British seamen, having had the experience of fourteen years of active seafaring to assess them, and as it turned out, his faith was fully justified.

Three days later, having taken on board fresh water and stores, the three ships set sail. It was the 12th of September, a Friday as it happened,[3] the course being set southwards for the Portuguese Cape Verde Islands. On the following day, Wallis sent a boat over to the *Swallow* with a copy of the orders for the voyage, including a rendezvous at Port Famine in the Straits of Magellan in the event of the ships becoming separated by bad weather or other causes. Altogether this was another leisurely passage, taking eleven days to cover the 800 miles to Porto Praya on the island of St Jago, the largest one of the Cape Verde archipelago, anchoring there on September 23rd.

This was a fertile little isle lying within the Tropic of Cancer and was a popular port of call for outward bound ships: here were supplies of cattle, sheep and pigs, also a good variety of fruit and vegetables necessary to stave off the effects of scurvy, and for the next four days, the three ships filled their water-casks and took on board further stores. This was to be the last contact with civilisation for the next fifteen months.

On the 27th September, they weighed anchor and made sail and now commenced the most pleasant part of the voyage, wafted on as they were by the north-east trades until they reached equatorial waters. Here the fluky winds and calms of the Doldrums slowed them down on occasion to a state of complete immobility until at last they found the South-East trades. Soon after this they entered the Southern Hemisphere, and now, sailing close-hauled on the port tack, their progress continued at

---

[3] Sailor's superstitions always believed Friday to be an unlucky day on which to sail.

a steady four or five knots. The *Swallow* had no chronometer[4] and for that matter neither did the other two ships and since no lunars were observed, the longitude was determined by dead reckoning: the latitude presented no problem since it could be calculated daily by an observation of the sun's meridian altitude.

Thus the little flotilla sailed on a course roughly parallel to the coast of South America until they reached the latitude of Rio Galegos, fifty miles north of the Straits of Magellan, in latitude 51°39 1/2' South. When this parallel was observed they altered course due west until they made their landfall. This method of navigation was known as "latitude sailing". From Rio Galegos they turned south towards Cape Virgin Mary at the entrance to the Straits of Magellan. During this period on the coast, Carteret was pleased to be able to make contact with native Patagonians. He barely mentions this in his Journal, but he wrote an account of his meeting with them which was read before the Royal Society at a later date. Also on this passage south the *Swallow* lost the first member of her crew, namely John Hendrik Crouch, a German seaman, one time native of Berlin. He died on December 2nd, 1766 and was buried at sea.

According to Carteret's Journal, this appears to have been a pleasant interlude. Nothing disturbed the tenor of this passage apart from his concern over the "ill quality of the ship and the manner in which she was equipped." It was a lengthy passage indeed, 80 days to traverse a distance of 4,500 mile after mile of ocean, an average of 55 per day. No doubt there were calms, contrary winds perhaps, and possibly a pampero, but he tells us nothing of this, only a gentle complaint of not having more officers with the Master Alexander Simpson being ill since Madeira and no other warrant officer to take his place. At last

---

[4] The chronometer was still in its infancy. Two years later Captain Cook sailed with one of Harrison's, the first to be used on a voyage of discovery.

on December 16th the three ships came to anchor off Cape Virgin Mary.

After ten weeks at sea the sight and scent of the land has a special charm to the seafarer, but they had only the briefest respite before entering the Strait. The early reaches presented the lesser difficulties: "the shore on both sides consists of level planes, parklike scenery and clear blue sky," wrote young Darwin on board the *Beagle* seventy years later. The real challenge was to come in the narrow parts beyond Cape Gregory some seventy miles into the Strait where the channels were confined and the winds predominantly adverse. Wallis had no experience of these waters, therefore he ordered Carteret to lead the way in the *Swallow* to act as pilot to the other two ships. In this respect his experience was invaluable, but the poor old *Swallow* was a sore trial and whatever adjustments were made regarding the masts since leaving England, none of it had improved her sailing qualities. In Carteret's own words, "seldom could we make her tack without the help of a boat to bring her round."

Altogether it took the flotilla nine days to reach Port Famine, a distance of little more than 150 miles. The hazards were many: rocks and sandbanks, mostly uncharted; strong tides with currents running at three to six knots that were very useful when favourable but requiring a hasty anchorage at the turn. All this made tedious by the unhandiness of the ship, needing the cutter to be always in the water fully manned at all times and ready to tow the heavy old ship around each time she missed stays. The more tricky parts were the two narrows named "First" and "Second" by the *Swallow's* purser, Edward Leigh who, in spite of his other duties concerning the ship's papers and accounts found time to make a chart of the Straits from Point Dungeness at the eastern end to Cap Pilar. These two reaches, each about ten miles long and two miles wide at the narrowest could be traversed in one tide if conditions happened to be right which however they rarely were. On the credit side Simpson had recovered, taking some of the load off Carteret's shoulders and it was decided to do something about the *Swallow's* sailing qualities at the first opportunity.

At last they came to anchor at Port Famine[5] on Friday December 26th. It was not really a port, merely an anchorage sheltered from the West. Previously there had been a Spanish settlement there but starvation had forced it to be abandoned, hence its name. It lies in 53°37'S 70°56'W situated roughly at a point halfway through the Strait. "I never saw a more cheerless prospect," wrote Darwin bluntly, but anyway it was summertime now, a fine place for wood, beech trees largely, water aplenty and soon the boats were plying to and fro replenishing their depleted stocks. It was also a good place for obtaining a plant similar to English celery which Carteret issued to his crew to combat scurvy which it did effectively. During their sojourn at this place, Carteret put his carpenters to work on an extension to the rudder for improved steering, no small matter as the rudder had to be unshipped and when this had been done, he had them erecting the wooden awning over the quarter-deck denied him by the Admiralty at home, which he considered very necessary for collecting rainwater. It was completed with timber cut from the shore and was to prove most useful since, even with all her casks full, the *Swallow* was short by twenty tons of what was required for reasonable endurance.

This was the parting of the ways for the *Prince Frederick*, but before she sailed both the *Dolphin* and *Swallow* took on board as much stores as they could stow. Every inch of space was filled, even the Captain's cabin was chock-a-block with bread and each member of the crew was given a month's ration of bread in advance to take care of as best they could. All this done, the *Prince Frederick* weighed anchor and set sail for Port

---

[5] Some years later a port was established 28 miles to the north called Punta Arenas which became a bunkering place for ships passing through the Straits and the centre of the wool trade in that area.

Egmont in the Falkland Islands. The date was January 16th, 1767: two days later, after twenty-three days at Port Famine, Captain Wallis gave the order for the remaining ships to make sail.

During the first day they made good progress rounding Cape Froward, a prominent headland with the peak of Mt. Victoria towering above, and coming to anchor off Cape Holland, a day's run of thirty miles. It was a deep disappointment however to find that for all the adjustments to mast, sails, draft and rudder, that the *Swallow's* sailing qualities had not improved one bit. Furthermore, if the terrain from Cape Virgin Mary to Port Famine was considered inhospitable and the navigation arduous in the extreme, it was to prove nothing in comparison to the desolate, barren and forbidding reaches which lay ahead. "Gloomy stretches of water", wrote a seasoned sailor, "acres of trailing kelp concealing sunken rocks, fierce willywaws shrieking down from snow-capped granite mountains"; even the names were enough to engender a feeling of dread in the mariner's heart, Port Famine, Cape Froward, Bay of Disappointment and the lonely fjords of Desolation Island.

Bearing all this in mind, Carteret penned a letter to Wallis on January 22nd informing him of the *Swallow's* continued unhandiness and that in such confined waters which lay ahead, he could not answer for the safety of the ship.

Wallis's reply was quite firm. "I have to inform you," he writes, "that as the Lord's Commissioners of the Admiralty have thought fit to order the *Swallow* on this service. I do not think myself at liberty to alter the sloop's said destination."

It was one of Carteret's failings that he never appeared to realise when to bow to the inevitable. Perhaps in some respects it was his strength, a trait which eventually carried him through the trials and hazards which lay ahead, but it was irritating to his superiors to have their orders or decisions frequently questioned. And now, having had no favourable answer to his communication he tried another tack, whether by letter or meeting he does not say. Yet there is no doubt that he was sincere in that the delay caused by the *Swallow's* unhandiness was jeopardising the success of the voyage. "I therefore proposed to Captain Wallis," he writes, "to lay the *Swallow* up in some cove then with her boats, I will see the *Dolphin* safe out of the Straits." In short, he would act as pilot. Other advantages in this scheme were that the *Dolphin* could have the benefit of the *Swallow's* provisions, stores and ship's company, after which she could return home.

Once again Wallis declined to consider this proposal and by now must have had quite enough, wishing only that Carteret would get on with his duties. It must have required all his patience when Carteret further proposed, with his knowledge of the Straits he would prepare to go as First Lieutenant of the *Dolphin* and pilot her through, while the *Dolphin's* Lieutenant could sail the *Swallow* home to England.

Wallis's answer was predictable, "as their Lordships had thought it necessary that two ships should go together he did not think it proper to alter their intentions."

This reply shows great forbearance on Wallis's part and one could be forgiven for assuming that this communication must be the last. But no, Carteret has one more word on the matter replying "that for my part, I was not afraid of going on this duty of a single ship, for if he would take the *Swallow* back to Europe and let me have the *Dolphin* (whose goodness I know) I made no doubt that I should be able to fulfil the intentions of the voyage."

What reply Wallis made to this is not recorded, but the continual delay prompted him to order both ships to be put on short allowance, two-thirds everything except 'grog' which he desired should be continued at full measure. The full grog ration was much appreciated but the reduction in provisions was particularly hard on the seamen who bore the brunt of the ship's hard work to hand, reef and steer, boxing the yards around on each successive tack, frequently having to tow her with the boats when she missed stays, or heaving their hearts out with those great heavy sweeps.

Chapter III

Thus, with the the *Swallow* as usual in the lead, the two ships set sail from Cape Holland. It was Sunday, January 18th as they commenced their tedious way up the wild unchanging wilderness of snow-capped granite mountains, first through Royal Reach into the aptly named Crooked Reach, barely a mile wide at its narrowest, bleak, barren, rock-girt stretches, thence into the slightly broader Long Reach. Every possible means was needed to be employed to make progress and now, since the *Swallow* was so foul and sluggish, the *Dolphin* was sometimes obliged to take her in tow. Therefore, it was not until March 17th that the two ships reached Upright Bay, a good anchorage, sheltered from the west some sixty miles distant from Cap Pilar. Here the two ships remained windbound at anchor for the next twenty-four days, while a succession of gales blew from the west, frustrating further immediate progress. At last on Friday, April 10th the long wait came to an end.

The dawn that day was cold and blustery, a grey gloomy start with squalls of snow and hail, "having all the appearance of Winter", wrote Carteret, but the wind which had kept them pinned down in the bay all this time swung round, a merciful, much longed for breeze blowing from the south-east and by 10 o'clock that morning anchors were aweigh, and both ships sheeting home their sails to a fair wind, their prows heading for the open sea.

The way ahead was now clear, open water as far as the eye could see, and the *Swallow*, a brave sight with all plain sail aloft, was making the best speed possible in the unsteady breeze. Yet in spite of this, the *Dolphin* with her copper bottom still clean, needed only reefed topsails to keep pace with her, and Wallis could be forgiven for any impatience with Carteret for his reluctance to set his studdingsails which he considered imprudent in view of the sudden squalls and the variable winds in the Straits of Magellan. However, he did risk the topmast stuns'ls to start with and even later further overcame his scruples by setting topgallant stuns'ls in an effort to make as much headway as possible while the east wind lasted.

By mid-afternoon both ships had cleared Tamar Island and at six o'clock that evening it was estimated that another twenty miles would see them in the Pacific Ocean itself. Yet progress was pitifully slow, three knots perhaps, until in the evening watch, those aboard the *Swallow* observed the *Dolphin* set her forecourse thus steadily increasing her lead. Then, as the evening progressed she drew further and further away until by nine o'clock she was lost to view in the gathering dusk and since she exhibited no lanterns, they saw nothing more of her that night.

No one on board the *Swallow* could blame the *Dolphin* for making the most of the fair wind. It was unlikely to last. Once clear of the Straits, she would no doubt wait for her consort or meet at a rendezvous in due course. After all, had not her Commander always insisted that their Lordships' instructions be carried out to the letter, that the two ships would remain together at all times. It was unthinkable that he should desert them after all their efforts. He had showed himself a good Commander, patient in the extreme over the *Swallow's* faults, considerate of the crew's welfare, especially over the grog ration. No, she would be there on the morrow, hove to waiting for them once she had made a good offing, of that they were certain.

All that night, a light breeze blew steadily from the East, which wafted the *Swallow* along under topgallant studlingsails. At 6 a.m. next morning, the quaintly named Westminster Hall

Island bore N&W 1/2 W 4 leagues giving the distance covered in the night watches a meagre 14 miles. The *Dolphin* as expected had done better sailing two more miles to the *Swallow's* but was still in sight hull down bearing WNW, sailing on regardless stuns'ls above and aloft until 9 o'clock, she was completely out of sight.

To Carteret, if not the rest of the crew, it appeared that they had been deserted by the *Dolphin* at a time when with good fortune they might have rejoined her, but it was not to be. At about noon, when the *Swallow* was abreast of Cap Pilar, the wind swung around to the south west. Down came the stunsl's the topsails were reefed and every effort was made to get windward, but try as they might to coast her to weather that rugged headland, she would not do it. After a couple of hours with nothing gained to windward, there was no choice for it but to turn back to find a safe anchorage and wait for another opportunity.

Evening was drawing in as they steered in as they steered back looking for Tuesday Bay. There was a gale blowing now with a heavy sea running, but in spite of this a boat was hoisted out and with Simpson in charge was sent ahead to guide them to the anchorage, but in the gloom, the wind and the rain she was quite hard to view and for some time there was much anxiety for her safety. During the long wait lanterns were hoisted, flares lit, even a signal gun fired every half hour until she returned at last without however finding anywhere to anchor.

The rest of the night was spent with the *Swallow* drifting around in great danger of going ashore beneath the cliffs, which were impossible to see in the darkness in spite of their great height. The wind remained in the south-west, eminently favourable for the *Dolphin*, and Carteret was under no illusions that Wallis would be making the most of it sailing away into the Pacific Ocean. The *Swallow's* crew were of the contrary opinion and their high regard and trust in their superior officers, were confident that very soon they would see the *Dolphin* sailing in rejoin them.

The next day was Sunday April 12th. At first light Simpson was sent with the cutter to find an anchorage where they could ride out the gales until a favourable shift of wind allowed them to leave these perilous waters where so much time and labour had been wasted. But finding a suitable mooring with good holding ground occupied the whole day until 6 o'clock before it was done. By now a gale was blowing with great gust which by nature of the high cliffs disturbed the surface of the water creating a whirling mist. Due to some trick of the light the lookout thought he spied a ship and in the heat of the moment sung out in deck "Sail ho!" which brought the whole crew rushing out on deck in a fever if expectation cheering wildly that the *Dolphin* had returned and their faith in Commodore Wallis had not been misled and that all would soon be as it was before.

Carteret, who had retired to the Great Cabin, on hearing the unexpected noise and excitement which echoed all through the ship with all hands rushing up on deck, imagined that the *Swallow* had parted her cables and was driving helplessly out of the bay. To his relief this was not the case but he found the crew in a state of utter dejection when they learnt that there was no ship.

But Carteret himself was by now convinced that they would never see their erstwhile consort again, and together with the rest of his crew, felt completely let down and ill-used by the Admiralty back home and Captain Wallis for deserting them. Sensing their utter dejection, he mustered the crew on deck and when they were gathered he spoke to them telling them that they must have no illusions about their situation, and that from now on the *Swallow* would be on her own. But in spite of this, he was confident that with their courage and behaviour they would emulate the *Dolphin's* achievements and show their King and Country that they were equal to any undertaking set them.

Strong words indeed and perhaps stronger than he felt himself, but they had the desired effect and, as he wrote in his Journal, that in spite of the present frustration and uncertain future, "never a ship's company behaved in a better manner whether in point of courage, obedience to their officers, or Steadiness in the most difficult Situations." On his part Carteret was satisfied by their attitude which they showed their implicit faith in him as their commander to persevere and continue the voyage alone.

It was well indeed that they did, since the problems which lay ahead might appear insurmountable to them: ten thousand miles of uncharted ocean to traverse before they would reach any semblance of civilisation where, apart from the dangers of storm, reef and scurvy the spears of hostile islanders would thin their ranks.

For Carteret himself, it was a time to take stock of his situation. The *Swallow*, intended primarily as a support ship to the *Dolphin* was an unhandy vessel, a slow sailer and far from suitable for a lone exploration over vast distances. She was short of stores, also trade goods[6] required to barter with natives for fresh food when she touched land.

Since the likelihood of meeting up with the *Dolphin* again was remote, there was a decision to be made on what course to take across the Pacific. It appears from Carteret's Journal, that there was little or no discussion between him and Wallis over this, but to a certain extent the prevailing winds were the governing factor. However, it was supposed that somewhere to the west lay a great continent, as most eminent geographers believed, and with this in view, instructions from the Admiralty

---

[6] A variety of items, cloth, knives, hatchets, trinkets, etc.

were clear; they were to make as much westing as possible between 100° to 120° of longitude from the Straits of Magellan in search of it. In the event of failure to discover the continent, a north-westerly course might be shaped to look for land or islands in this direction.

To sail due west, as required by the Admiralty, needed a well-found, weatherly ship able to make long tacks over great distances, something which no explorer had attempted and which the *Swallow* was quite unsuited. But now, the first task was to coax the old ship out of the straits into the open sea. For the moment, however, there was no chance of this; the gale continued and although Carteret was uneasy with the anchorage he had no choice but to wait for moderation.

Monday, April 13th saw the *Swallow* pinned down in the same berth. Tuesday was even worse; a succession of violent and intense little depressions assailed them with the wind boxing the compass from WSW to SSE and back again. Each time it blew from the SE the crew, on Carteret's order, manned the capstan and prepared to make sail, the wind being fair for Cap Pilar, only to be frustrated as it veered round to the south-west again. On the second attempt to get under weigh, the wind came shrieking down on them at hurricane force which, although favourable, no canvas could stand, bringing with it the immediate danger of moorings parting and the ship driving on the rocks. Amidst the tumult of the willywaw and the driving, blinding rain and hail, another anchor was hurriedly dropped and more cable veered out with all hands set to hoisting the cutter aboard and sending down the topgallant masts and yards, no easy task under those conditions in order to get the ship snugged down as well as possible.

The storm reached its height about noon and continued with lightning and deluges of rain until late that night, when at about midnight on Wednesday, April 15th it unexpectedly moderated and blew from the south-east. Not wishing to miss such a good opportunity in spite of the uncertainty of the weather, the capstan was manned to get under weigh directly while the wind favoured. But now, as Kerton recounted in his log, one of the cables became foul of a rock, and heave as the seamen might, they could not break the anchor out, not even with additional purchase. However, a lucky squall caused the *Swallow* to take a sudden sheer clearing the anchor, which was quickly hove up; then, while some of the crew fished, catted and stowed it, others speedily hoisted sail and soon were making four knots towards the open sea.

By six bells in the graveyard watch the wind had dropped away, but this gave Carteret the opportunity to have the topgallant masts hoisted, yards crossed and more sail set. Soon after this the wind freshened even further with the *Swallow* making five, even six knots by the log, the wind now so strong that the topgallant masts and yards had to be struck again. Nonetheless she was still much overpressed and according to Kerton's log she was shipping heavy seas which continually flooded the deck causing dire apprehension that she might founder at any moment. Water casks, stowed on top for want of space in the hold cluttered up the deck impeding the seamen as they tried to haul on the braces and halliards, while the extra weight appeared to bear the ship down making her cranky. In view of this, orders were given to stave the casks and throw them overboard together with some lumber and other obstructions, while a further number of casks stowed in the 'tween decks were staved and the contents pumped overboard, a desperate measure considering the value of drinking water at all times. In spite of all this the *Swallow* continued to run before the storm and early in the morning watch Cap Pilar was observed bearing SW by W a distance of two miles off with the crew in high spirits to be at last clear of the dark cliffs and treacherous tide-rode waters of the Straits of Magellan.

It had taken them four months of unremitting toil to navigate the *Swallow* from Cape Virgins to Cap Pilar. Captain Fitzroy in the *Beagle* did it in four days, thirty-five years later. But be that as it may, all that was behind them, and by noon the *Swallow* had run some 48 miles by the log since leaving Tuesday Island to a position 6 leagues to the westward of the Evangelistas, islands known particularly to British seamen as the Isles of Direction, and it seemed that all their troubles were over with the broad endless expanse of the Pacific Ocean before them and the prospect of calmer seas and warmer climes to come: time to relax, time for the steady routine of "watch and watch" to take over. Carteret found time to note the variety of sea birds: albatross, gannets, sheerwaters, Cape Pigeons and petrels known to sailors as Mother Carey's chickens.

But before setting course into the Pacific, Carteret needed to address the problem of finding somewhere to refill the empty casks in the hold. With this in mind, he decided to make for the lonely island of Juan Fernandez[7] which, as far as he knew was uninhabited and where the *Dolphin* had wood and watered on his previous voyage under Byron's command.

Of the next seven days Carteret has very little to say in his Journal. There were no calamities at any rate and the crew were able to settle down to a steady routine as the *Swallow* steered towards Juan Fernandez. Turning to Kerton's log we read that the topgallant masts were raised, the yards crossed and the sails sheeted home to take advantage of the favourable breeze. This was Thursday, April 16th, a quiet day's sailing with the distance by the log streamed and recorded every hour added up to a mere forty-seven miles from noon to noon. There were whales

---

[7] This island, 400 miles off the coast of Chile, was generally known to British seamen as John Fernandes Island. Dampier refers to it by that name. The Spanish called it Mas-a-Tierra. One hundred miles west lies the island of Mas-Afuera. On British Admiralty Chart 4007, it comes under the heading of Juan Fernandez Archipelago, Alexander Selkirk Island to the west and Robinson Crusoe Island to the east, the latter made famous by Daniel Defoe. The Chileans still give it the name of Robinson Crusoe Island.

around, also seabirds aplenty, some of which the crew caught with hook and line, particularly one species described by Kerton as a beautiful black and white bird about the size of a pigeon, which he said was very good eating.

Friday brought more wind and a nasty confused swell, but the day's run was better, 81 miles; while on Saturday, with stuns'ls alow and aloft the old ship logged 112 miles. From Sunday onwards progress was slow, 50 miles per day, during which the sailmaker was employed making new main topgallant stuns'ls while the crew, when not tending the sails, were employed drawing and knotting yarns or pointing the ends of cables; on occasion they were exercised at the Great Guns and small arms. The cooper occupied his time repairing and assembling his casks ready for replenishment at Juan Fernandez: by now most of them were empty and the loss of weight at the bottom of the ship, amounting to twenty or more tons, reduced the *Swallow's* stability, hence the need for sending down the fore and main topgallant yards and masts when the wind blew strongly. The boatswain and his mates attended to the rigging, replacing worn cordage and setting up shrouds and backstays. They also played an important part in dealing with the topgallant masts and yards when they had to be struck. Such an evolution can be carried out alongside a quay-wall without difficulty but in a sea-way, it is another matter and that it was done in all kinds of weather aboard the *Swallow* is a credit to the seamanship of the crew.

With regard to the navigation with the grey lowering weather of those latitudes, fixing the ship's position with any accuracy was limited to 'dead reckoning' and when possible a latitude obtained by observation of the sun's meridian altitude. Navigational instruments were limited to the compass and quadrant, Harrison's chronometer still being in its infancy, and neither Carteret nor his officers practised finding the longitude by observing the lunar distance, a long, tedious calculation which required a set of tables predicting the moon and certain fixed stars. Thus the *Swallow*, like most ships of her day, was navigated by the time honoured method of log, lead and lookout, a method somewhat hazardous at times needing all a seaman's instincts to be successful.

The Roaring Forties are no easy waters for a small unhandy ship and the shifts in wind which came so frequently in those latitudes would try Carteret's skill and seamanship to the limit and also those of his crew. The lack of a barometer, that valuable instrument invented by Terricelli in 1643, but not yet in general use at sea, deprived him of the means of predicting changes in the weather, particularly sudden shifts of wind which for ever plagued him catching the poor old *Swallow* unawares, threatening to bring the masts down around the crew's ears. Then there were times, too frequent in fact, when favoured by moderate winds, the topgallant masts and yards were sent up only to be struck again almost immediately when hit unexpectedly by a gale; and perhaps equally trying was her reluctance to tack, even with unrestricted sea room to do so. It happened all too frequently and Kerton's log reveals this. One such day was April 26th, a special day perhaps, being Sunday, as he starts the day by noting that the crew were issued with tobacco, but certainly no day of rest: the wind then blowing from the north-west required that the *Swallow* be on the port tack; accordingly at six bells in the morning watch with the crew at stations, the helm was put down and she was brought to the wind. But she would not have it however hard they tried to make her, and it was a case of up helm and bring her round on the other tack by wearing. Later, when the wind veered, they tried again to make her tack but once more she was caught in stays and had to be brought round with the wind aft.

Monday found the *Swallow* some 500 miles nearer Juan Fernandez: any day now she would be leaving the stormy latitudes with the expectation of improving weather to come. But as it turned out, that evening was a particularly black one for her and the crew. She was steering to the westward under courses and close-reefed main-topsail, when the wind came unheralded out of the darkness from right ahead, bringing the ship all aback in a trice, laying over almost on her beam ends while the crew struggled to get the sails off her, an almost impossible task with wet canvas clinging to the masts. But at last they succeeded in clewing up the mainsail and main-topsail and getting the ship to pay off before the wind. All that night they scudded northwards while the wind favoured them, but on Wednesday about noon, it dropped away leaving the *Swallow* at the mercy of a high, confused swell which assailed her from all directions causing her to roll so violently that they feared that the masts must go overboard. This perilous situation continued until the end of the first dog watch, when the wind came fair from the WSW and now under great press of sail, the course was again set to the north.

All that day and next morning they ran before the storm and by noon on Thursday, the last day of April, she had reached latitude 41°50'S, 480 miles from Juan Fernandez. However, this was too good to continue with the wind once again coming at them from the NW blowing with such force that sail had to be reduced.

So it went on day after day, a continual battle to make progress northward, days and nights of northerly winds and gales sometimes reaching hurricane strength, boxing the compass from north to south time and time again, catching the *Swallow* aback, sending her over on her beam ends, pinning her down in great danger of foundering or at least dismasting. There were periods of calm which left her in a cauldron of giant toppling waves assailing her from all directions, sweeping over her like a half-tide rock, the decks hardly ever clear of water. At times like this Carteret had good reason to bless the forward and after bulkheads he had caused to be constructed in Chatham, which kept the seas from invading the hull. Many times he feared that she would not survive such an onslaught, but survive she did, storm after storm and in the end he had to admit "that she was an extraordinary good seaboat, which was the only good quality she had." He remarked particularly, almost with affection, how "wonderfully well this little vessel rose and cleared herself from these mountainous seas."

However, the damage wreaked by these storms was mounting: several chain-plates and deadeyes which secured the shrouds to the hull were broken, also a rudder chain carried away; the gaff, a spar at the head of the fore-and-aft sail on the mizzen-mast, was broken in two, and six sweeps or heavy oars used to propel the ship during calms, were lost when a mighty sea broke over the quarter. After such a night as this with all hands continually on deck and the ship in imminent danger of foundering, Carteret, always considerate of the crew's morale under such conditions, ordered a dram of rum to cheer them on and set them up for further exertions to come.

The first week in May brought weather conditions much the same with gales, calms and adverse winds. When the wind did favour them, sail was piled on and the *Swallow* put on course for Juan Fernandez and the opportunity taken to repair the rigging using whatever means they had at hand. The want of a forge, denied by the Admiralty in Chatham and deplored by Carteret, was now keenly felt since so much of the ship's ironwork became damaged, particularly in way of the chainplates. Even so, some sort of forge complete with firebox and bellows must have been contrived, seamen being so amazingly ingenious when put to the test, since repairs to the chainplates were effected together with the rudder chains. During the lulls the sailmaker stitched and patched up the sails and the bosun and his men, assisted by the carpenter, repaired the gaff by scarfing the two parts together. In other ways conditions improved; the *Swallow* permitted herself to be tacked without getting in stays.

On Friday, May 8th the wind came away from the south bringing good weather with it. The topgallant masts and yards were sent up, the sails set and away went the *Swallow* steering due north and logging five, sometimes six and a half knots. The next day at dawn, the latitude by meridian altitude of Capella was calculated to be 35°16' South with the breeze gradually falling away and the speed with it. The weather was particularly fine and all hands were ordered to get their hammocks on deck for an airing and the lower deck cleared up, the first opportunity of doing this for three months. In the middle of it all land was sighted, not Juan Fernandez as it turned out, but the island of Mas Afuera ninety miles to the west, Carteret being that much out in the reckoning of his longitude. This was no great miscalculation under the circumstances, but a meridian altitude of the sun put the *Swallow* sixty miles southward of Mas Afuera while Kerton, in his log states at the same time he saw "the looming of the Island of Juan Fernandez bearing NE by N about 30 leagues," only a seaman's instinctive hunch since no sighting was possible not even from the masthead. However the course was altered to NE, and the following afternoon, Sunday, brought Juan Fernandez in sight where a great disappointment awaited Carteret and indeed the whole crew.

That afternoon as the *Swallow* sailed towards what all hands hoped would be a safe haven for a well-earned rest, the crew prepared the anchors and shackled on the cables in readiness. This being Sunday a cask of salt meat was specially opened for the crew's dinner. Kerton records it in detail no. 1145 with 322 pieces of salt meat in it. The crew were also issued with vinegar that day. Next morning at eleven, Goat Island was abeam three leagues, and by the afternoon, the wind being fair, the course was set round the eastern shore of this green and pleasant island making for Cumberland Bay where there was a good anchorage. Both Anson and Byron had called there before continuing their voyage across the Pacific. It was also visited by other adventurers; pirates, buccaneers and all the riffraff of the oceans and had been so for a century or more. It was also a handy place where troublesome unwanted crew could be marooned. Here was everything available for the mariner; all the fruit, fresh meat, fish and fowl he could desire together with a temperate climate, wooded hills, sheltered valleys with green pastures. Anson in particular, when he was there in 1741 viewed it as an ideal place for provisioning ships and recuperating crews suffering from scurvy, even going as far as to sow carrots, lettuces and other seeds, also planting out apricot, plum and peach stones for future use by mariners. Goats thrived there, and seals and sea-lions thronged the beaches to provide meat which could be salted down to supplement the seamen's diet of pork and beef.

But to return to the *Swallow*, on clearing the eastern shore, she hauled her wind in order to beat into Cumberland Bay. It became immediately apparent to all on board that the island was no longer uninhabited. On the foreshore a large number of men were observed, two score or more, certainly not shipwrecked mariners, but soldiers, armed and hostile: furthermore on a hill dominating the bay was a building, no temporary structure by the look of it, but a fort of some substance, stone-built with twenty embrasures for guns. Above all this flew the flag of Spain. Two large boats were anchored off the beach.

As the *Swallow* made her approach, the sight of these defences, particularly the cannons on the foreshore covering the approaches, warned Carteret that very soon they would be within range, and although as far as he knew Spain was not at war with Britain, he was well aware of their dislike of any encroachment into their domains. Not wishing to be blown out of the water he hoisted no colours and bore away out of range.

Once clear of those menacing cannons the course was set to close the western end of the bay for a further scrutiny of the Spanish occupation. Any information regarding this would be welcome at the Admiralty and in due course to other seamen, but the wind, blowing straight off the land at gale force, frequently caused the tops'l sheets to be let fly in a hurry in spite of their being close-reefed, and the *Swallow*, never a weatherly ship at any time, could not be coaxed deeper into the bay. However, they managed to open up West Bay which lies further along the coast where a guardhouse and two cannons were observed close by the beach. Having seen all he wanted, Carteret wore ship onto the other tack and stood once more for Cumberland Bay as if intending to go in, at which a boat put off from the shore for some purpose, friendly or otherwise. But Carteret, not wishing to make contact with them, did not tarry, maintaining an easterly course while he pondered his next move. The boat continued to follow them until sunset when they soon lost sight of her.

Chapter IV

The occupation of Juan Fernandez was a harsh blow to Carteret's plans, since not only was his need for water urgent but he had expected to be able to give his crew a run ashore, a chance to relax from the hardships of the Magellan passage and to obtain fresh food with which to combat scurvy. To land there under the existing circumstances was out of the question: the less the Spanish knew about his affairs and the purpose of his voyage the better, although the general appearance of the *Swallow* must have left them in little doubt. She was no merchant ship for certain, and by the look of her, too taut and shipshape for a pirate or buccaneer. Undoubtedly they would know that she was a warship, albeit an inferior one, and in spite of showing no colours, probably British. Their ships were coming more and more frequently to the Pacific, planting their flag on remote islands and looking for that great continent said to exist in the South Pacific Ocean.

Carteret was now faced with the alternative of retracing his steps ninety miles west to Mas Afuera.[8] Anson had recommended it as a possible option if Juan Fernandez was denied them. Carteret himself had been there with Commodore Byron when he was First Lieutenant in the *Dolphin*. Fortunately

---

[8] Mas Afuera is shown on Admiralty charts as Isla Alejandro Selkirk.

the Spanish regarded it as little more than a heap of rocks and placed no garrison there. Accordingly he set the *Swallow's* course west or as near to it as the wind permitted her to sail.

Adverse wind and weather continued to prevail with the *Swallow* on a taut bowline making slow progress: not until two days later did she cover the ninety miles separating the islands. It was Sunday, May 12th as she approached Mas Afuera.

That morning at six bells in the middle watch, although still dark, the peak of the island was sighted bearing west, an estimated distance of between nine and ten leagues. At daylight, the wind being favourable, the topgallant masts and yards were hoisted and all sail made with the *Swallow* logging between three and five knots. At 8 o'clock, with the island some four miles to windward, it was time to look for a suitable anchorage.

Mas Afuera is a small rocky island five and a half miles in length from north to south and three and a quarter miles across at its widest. The Peak, named Co de los Inocentes, rises to a height of 5,032 ft completely dominating the island and is the source of a number of streams cascading down to the coast. Anchoring presented no problem if a lee could be found, but only one good landing place existed for getting wood and water: this lay on the eastern side at Punta Langlois[9] where there was a berth with reasonable holding ground in eight to ten fathoms. However, with the wind from the north-east this could not be considered so the *Swallow's* course was set round the south of the island looking for a suitable alternative.

After breakfast, the cutter was hoisted out and with Simpson, the *Swallow's* Master in charge, was sent off to find a suitable

---

[9] Admiralty chart names the islet Ra del Sandalo.

anchorage on the western side while the *Swallow* fetched after her, keeping well in sight at a respectable distance offshore for fear of hidden reefs. They had been gone barely an hour when the lookout on the *Swallow* reported a ship ahead apparently under sail rounding the point, although there was no signal from the cutter. There was great excitement about this: was it a Spanish warship to bar their way or the *Dolphin* at last come to rejoin them? Who could say? But no, it was no more than a figment of the lookout's imagination, a small islet close by the shore with the sea breaking over it.

By the time they rounded the point, Punta Vicente Porras by name, giving it a wide berth in case of reefs, the cutter was still in sight running before the wind steering to the north, when at 2 o'clock, it was observed flying a signal that she had found an anchorage. Two hours later the *Swallow* hove to and came to a mooring with the best bower in twenty-two fathoms on fine black sand between two and three miles from the beach, a safe distance in case the wind changed putting her on a dangerous lee shore. If circumstances permitted, Carteret hoped to remain at this berth for as long as it might take to obtain wood and water, repair the rigging and spars damaged during the recent storms, and in general prepare the ship for the long voyage across the Pacific. In view of this, two sheet anchors were carried out to improve the moorings.

Now was the time to study the island in some detail, particularly the landing place. Mas Afuera, although small, appeared to have all that Carteret required for his needs: it was rocky, but with sufficient pasture, as he recorded in his Journal, for the "prodigious number of goats running about," and also "trees fit for firewood" for the galley. There were seals or sea lions which could be killed for meat, or blubber to be reduced to oil for various needs, and the water teemed with fish of all sorts. The landing place appeared to be suitable, situated as it was in a little sandy bay about a mile wide with a stream running through it. In fact, everything looked promising, so wasting no time at all, work commenced with part of the crew put to striking the topgallant masts and yards while the cutter and long boat were sent off for wood and water.

It was 6 o'clock, only an hour or two before dark, and as far as getting water the boats found that in spite of the shelter afforded by the bay, the surf was too great to permit them to land. But at any rate their time was not wasted: before returning to the sloop they had caught sufficient fish to feed the crew full and plenty; coley, halibut, rock cod and dog fish to name a few, a marvellous change of diet from salt junk and dried peas. There were also crayfish which was no doubt much enjoyed by Carteret.

Next morning, Thursday, even before daybreak, the boats were sent off to explore the northern part of the island for water. On board the *Swallow* the bosun and his mates put the crew to work setting up the topmast shrouds; they also renewed the catharpings while others bent a new foretopsail and fore-course. Two men were put ashore to kill seals and render their blubber down to oil for the ship's lamps. Others were landed to fill water barrels.

While all this work was going on, the boats, in spite of all their efforts, were having little success over water; although they managed to find some, the streams were reduced to a trickle due to the dry weather. They returned to the sloop at noon to repeat this. In the meantime, the men landed to shoot seals for blubber had no problems as they were so numerous and docile, and the goats they encountered were also unafraid but only one was shot, to be later pronounced fat and good eating. The boats were sent off again after dinner for water but returned with only four barrels. This was a disappointment to Carteret who had expected better.

However, on the brighter side, the weather had remained fair, the anchorage had afforded time to relax and have some much needed work carried out on sails and rigging; even better, the wind now appeared to be veering with the possibility of finding more suitable conditions for watering on the other side of the island.

Friday morning brought the change in the wind which gradually veered from east through south to south-west. At 5 a.m. Carteret gave the order to weigh anchor, the sails were sheeted home and the course set north about the island. On the passage round, there seems to have been an air of pleasant optimis, .it comes through in Kerton's log, the short spell at anchor with its relatively restful break in routine seemed to promise better things ahead. This may have had something to do with it.

The boats, which had already been on another fruitless errand for water, were dispatched to bring back the shore parties of waterers and sealers. When the anchor was aweigh, the *Swallow* stood to the north east keeping within a mile of the coast with the deep-sea lead going in the chains and the leadsman calling the depths: 20 fathoms, 30 fathoms, sometimes more, with the arming showing black sand. At 9 a.m. the boats caught up with them bringing the shore parties clambering aboard, no doubt pleased to be back among their shipmates. They also brought back one barrel of seal oil. Round about eleven, the *Swallow* passed the north-easternmost point of the island two cables off Cabo Norte with the hand lead going in shallow water. A shark seized the lead and hung on to it while the hands tried to bring the brute aboard where it would have been hacked to death with great glee, knowing the sailors hatred of sharks. All went well until it was half way up the ship's side when it let go, leaving the lead all gashed and chewed up and the crew mortally disappointed.

Not until 4 p.m. did the *Swallow* reach Punta Langlois where she anchored on a sand bank in 20 fathoms between two and three cables from the shore. This was a familiar place to Carteret who had been there before in the *Dolphin*, and all being well two or three days should see their water stocks to full capacity.

No time was wasted in dispatching the boats ashore. The cutter was soon back alongside with fifteen barrels, a good start which promised well. She was immediately sent off again with Lieutenant Gower in charge, his duty being to land and organise the shore party, some to cut wood, others to fill barrels. Their orders were to remain ashore to keep filling the barrels while the boats plied to and fro carrying full ones, at the same time ensuring that there was always empties available. For this purpose the shore party were supplied with rations. They also took some old sails to make themselves a shelter in case they had to stay overnight, a jolly change in routine and altogether quite a lark for them.

All in all, watering ship was no easy chore: landing places without surf were hard to find; wherever they searched, whichever way the wind blew, it was always the same with the risk of the boat being swamped or overturned. To reduce the risk of this, each boat had swimmers on board to dive in through the breakers ahead of the boat to drag her safely to the beach. The barrels, when full, each weighed 360 lbs, as much as four men could lift into the boat, while their presence on board impeded the oarsmen as they rowed back to the sloop to be hoisted or parbuckled aboard with the boat bumping and surging alongside. A calm sea was a rarity at this time of year, and since the island offered a poor lee, the boats were often in trouble.

This evening the wind was freshening from the north-west but not too strong to prevent the cutter being sent for water. It was 7 o'clock, and an hour later the long boat was sent off to catch fish which she did successfully, bringing back enough for all hands for a couple of days. It was midnight when she returned to the *Swallow*, and by then a gale was brewing up, blowing in hard gusts and lashing rain straight off the land and a sea getting up. By the look of it the crew could expect a rough night of it. And so it was.

Those that managed to get some sleep during those early

hours were woken up from their slumbers by the sound of the *Swallow* dragging her anchors and driving off the bank. Then it was all hands on deck with a vengeance to man the capstan, the messengers and nippers, in order to bring the anchors home before they parted their cables. By the time they had done this and sheeted home the tops'ls close-reefed, they were drifting to leewards fast, and try as they would to coax the *Swallow* to windward she would not have it, refusing to tack, forcing the crew to wear her each time. But at last the wind eased off a little, but the sea remained rough. Nonetheless, the boats were on their way ashore for water by 8 o'clock.

Two hours later the cutter returned with ten barrels, but not the long boat. This indeed was worrying. Nonetheless the cutter was sent off again. This time she also failed to return when expected and there was still no sign of the long boat. Some time later, much to Carteret's relief, they were both spotted lying to grapnels close to shore in what shelter they could find.

As far as getting any quantity of water aboard, it was an unprofitable day. The wind was still piping, a moderate gale in fact, with a rough sea and driving rain, but later in the day, Carteret managed to bring the sloop closer in, and after dinner the boats were glimpsed through the rain scudding before the wind along the shore towards Punta Negra at the south-east corner of the island. The *Swallow* bore down to the point and signalled them to come alongside, which they did with some difficulty, receiving a good bit of damage before they were hoisted aboard.

It was a great disappointment to find that they had brought the barrels back empty, the surf being too high to land them, and the damage to the boats was serious, keeping the carpenters busy all night repairing them so as to have them ready for work first thing next morning.

The following day, Sunday May 17th, events were much the same with a great deal of effort going in towards getting water, but in fact very little being achieved. The *Swallow*, having lain hove to that night under balanced mizen, made sail at 4 a.m. in order to close the land. The wind never seemed to let up, and this morning was blowing as fresh as ever, but being westerly off the land, did not bring too great a sea. However, the old *Swallow* was in one of her sulky moods and would not stay, so the cutter was launched to tow her round and soon after this had been done, she was sent off for water with Lieutenant Gower in charge.

The cutter was gone an unusually long time and did not show up again until late afternoon with the *Swallow* standing on and off as near to the shore as possible. The time however was not wasted. The captain of the hold and his party, so Kerton tells us in his log, were down below re-stowing and filling up the empty tuns.

At 4 p.m. Lieutenant Gower brought the cutter back with a full load of water and the news that the shore party had passed a bad night, and during the storm had lost several casks. Up until now they had been having a taste of the good life under canvas away from the discipline of the ship and feasting on as much freshly killed goat's meat as they could eat. The storm which drove the *Swallow* off the bank hit the little valley where they camped and watered, bringing a heavy downpour of rain turning the stream into a raging torrent which swept away and smashed the casks, with the seamen nearly sharing the same fate. However, all was well now and another load of barrels would be ready to bring back at any time.

Carteret was against this. It was too late in the day and the weather was uncertain. But Gower, on his way back from the landing place, had observed some runnels in full spate within easy access. The *Swallow* by now had closed the shore, and he considered that a load of barrels could be quickly filled and the cutter brought back alongside in good time. In the end, Carteret agreed.

The weather changed almost immediately after Gower left. A black cloud looming over the Mount of the Innocents was lit by flashes of flickering lightning. Then came rain, blotting out the land and seascape, at the same time reducing the cutter's chance of sighting the *Swallow* at any distance in the gathering gloom. By now, the *Swallow* had drifted a long way to leewards leaving a stretch of four, maybe five miles of turbulent water for the cutter to traverse. It was 7 o'clock and darkness had already set in.

But where was the cutter after all this time? Sheltering perhaps; or was she tossing about in the rising sea and in considerable danger? The former conjecture was to be hoped for, but in case Gower had decided to take his chance and return at all costs, Carteret ordered flares to be lit and a swivel gun fired at frequent intervals.

Hopes were fading when at last she was seen, running before the storm, steering for the *Swallow's* lee, not a moment too soon as it turned out, with the gale rising fast. No time wasted in hoisting her in, a purchase from the mainyard, painters fore and aft to steady her, and bowsing lines to heave her inboard, a job for all hands. But even as the crew laboured to get her safe on the booms, a violent squall from the WNW laid the ship over almost on her beam ends, and Carteret noted in his Journal, "had we been half a minute later in getting the boat in we unavoidably must have lost her." As it was, the volume of the wind carried away the *Swallow's* mizen gaff and at the same time, a futtock plate on the main shrouds fractured. This obliged Carteret to order all sail to be furled immediately and allow the ship to lie to under bare poles, while the storm raged with great rolls of thunder, and lightning flashing all round the compass.

As soon as Gower had the opportunity to speak to Carteret, he had to report that he had not only failed to get any water but he had been forced to leave some of the cutter's crew on shore. This was bad news. They were three of the best seamen, swimmers from the Madeira episode who had braved the breakers ahead of the cutter to help guide her onto the beach, when suddenly the weather worsened, bringing with it a heavy surf, too great to allow him to fetch them off immediately. He was loathe to leave them and remained hove to clear of the surf in the hope that he might rescue them shortly, but with the sea rising and darkness setting in it proved impossible. In the end, he had to abandon them leaving all three in a pretty desperate situation with no food, no shelter and worst of all, no clothes, having discarded them before swimming ashore. True, there was food and shelter at the camp at Punta Langlois but it was doubtful if they could find their way there in the dark.

By midnight on Monday May 18th, the storm had blown itself out with the wind sufficiently moderated for Carteret to order the topsails and courses to be set, and in the early hours of the morning watch, the carpenters were put to work repairing the boats and fashioning a new gaff out of the spar of an old jibboom; they also repaired the broken futtock shroud. The wind was still fresh from the west and the end of the watch found the *Swallow* ten miles to leewards of the island, the set and drift of the tide, together with her leeway having put her there. With the breeze still fresh from the west, the next few hours were spent trying to regain the land.

The afternoon passed with nothing achieved in the way of obtaining further water, but now the *Swallow* had come close to the landing place at Punta Langlois where, in a short time, watering might be expected to be resumed. At this juncture, the breeze faded away to a calm, and in order to make some progress, Carteret ordered the cutter, although not completely repaired, to be hoisted out to tow the *Swallow* to the anchorage, and this was done. However, she had barely moved her any distance when the breeze returned wafting her offshore again, to spend another night under way.

With boats still under repair no water was fetched that evening, but the cutter, when eventually put right, was sent to the landing place to bring the three castaways back. Their captain was mighty relieved to see them safe aboard and ordered that they should be given some drink and allowed to lay in all night. Later, when the account of their night on shore was told, it turned out to be a harrowing one, yet the seamen involved, hard cases all three of them, suffered no ill effects in spite of their trials. When the cutter failed to return for them that night, they knew that they were in for a bad time of it with no clothes, no food and no means of lighting a fire or erecting a shelter. Also, it was raining hard. The watering party's camp at Punta Langlois was not far up the coast, no more than two miles, but the terrain was rocky with deep gullies which were impossible to negotiate in the dark. The prospect was bleak. However, they made the best of it by huddling together for warmth taking it in turn to lie on top. At daylight they set off for the camp scrambling along the shore, the only accessible way, until barred by rocky outcrops when they had to take to the water, swimming some distance beyond the surf, always running the risk of being taken by sharks. When they reached the camp, weary and famished, they were welcomed by their shipmates who gave them what clothes they could spare and shared their provisions with them. It was well for Carteret that he had such men as these among his crew. They were the backbone of the ship and he appreciated them, "My bold and fearless Madeira swimmers," he called them.

They were back on duty next day lending a hand to bring the *Swallow* to an anchorage. Circumstances were much the same with the ship having been set seven or eight miles to leewards of the island after a night of calms and light breezes. The cutter, the only boat in a fit state of repair, was sent off for water at 6 a.m., a long pull for her crew and did not return until midday. Meanwhile, the topgallant masts and yards were sent up and sail made in order to close the shore and bring her to an anchorage. Every effort was being made to overcome her reluctance to do this, sometimes tacking, on other occasions wearing when she missed stays. Kerton wrote quite scathingly of the old ship in his log that at times she lost more distance than she gained. Even Carteret himself was constrained to refer to her in his Journal as "this miserable tool", and as luck would have it, when she at last approached the anchorage and it appeared that all would be well, the breeze failed just as it did the day before, and she drifted off. However, the time was not wasted: the cutter returned with water and at 3 o'clock was sent off for another load. She succeeded in getting this without trouble and, into the bargain returned with enough fish to feed the whole ship's company. It was late and pitch dark as she made her way back and flares were lit and guns fired to guide her in. By the end of the second dog watch the wind started to pipe again with squalls and rain. Carteret wrote in his Journal, "that they had another foul night of it."

Next morning, Wednesday May 20th, a brisk NNW wind allowed Carteret an opportunity to reach the anchorage off Punta Langlois. Long boards of three to four leagues on a taut bowline were the order of the day for the *Swallow*, out on the port tack and back on the starboard. The wind was fresh, gale force at times, so at the end of the outward leg, with two reefs in the fore and mizen topsails, the crew had to wear her, but on the return she obliged them all by turning into the wind under the lee of the land without getting caught in stays.

It was noon when the best bower finally went down at the anchorage in eighteen fathoms. The cutter was then launched with Simpson in charge to sound around and carry out a kedge, and when this was done, the sloop was comfortably moored two cables offshore.

It was too late to send ashore for water but the longboat was hoisted out and put to fishing close in shore where the catch was particularly good, returning with plenty for all hands including a 'King Fish' weighing 88 lbs. By the time the longboat was hoisted in and stowed on board, the wind had begun to pipe again and once more the *Swallow* and her crew were in for a foul night.

By early morning Thursday, the wind veered four points to

the NNE and continued to blow all through the middle watch with the crew expecting the ship to be dragged ashore or off the bank. In the end, after paying out 200 fathoms, the *Swallow* was brought up. The wind backed north-westerly again, leaving her in an uncomfortable position, but at least safe from dragging ashore. The wind, however, continued at gale force with rain deluging down, rough sea and heavy surf and no possibility of getting water. As a precaution, the hawser on the kedge anchor was brought round the *Swallow's* stem, man-handled aft and made fast to the larboard quarter, all this done to give the ship a cast to starboard if the bower cable parted or had to be cut. By 8 p.m. the wind eased sufficiently and with the ship out of immediate danger and safe enough for three men to be put ashore to kill seals for oil.

Friday saw good progress bringing water on board, not that there was much improvement in the weather. There was still plenty of wind and the surf continued to run high. Nonetheless, conditions were as good as they could expect with a short pull to the beach for the boats and swimmers ready to bring them through the surf, while the watering party filled barrels as fast as they could be brought ashore. Then it was back to the *Swallow*, rolling uneasily at her moorings while the crew swayed the barrels aboard with a will, as anxious as anybody to get away from this godforsaken island. Under the circumstances, inevitably some barrels were stove in and their contents lost. There was a sense of urgency, of an opportunity not to be lost, and by the evening stocks were just about complete, nearly 40 tuns according to Kerton, only a few further barrels required, also some wood to get aboard for the galley and the shore party brought back. But this would have to be done the next day.

There was one windfall in the way of food. During the storm the previous night, as the watering party sat round their camp fire, a large number of sea birds, 500 or more attracted by the light, flew blindly into the flames. They were pindatos, considered good eating by the sailors who gathered them up to be sent aboard for the cooks to deal with.

The night of Saturday May 23rd, was a restless one for Carteret, the weather having all the appearance of another storm brewing. Because of this, the cutter and longboat were sent off to the landing place while it was still dark to bring back the last of the barrels and firewood. This did not take long, both boats returning by 7 o'clock, and having put the barrels on board were immediately sent off again to bring back the watering party together with the tent and other gear. Now that the watering was completed, Carteret was anxious to be gone.

The expectation of the boat's prompt return after loading up the equipment together with the last of the firewood was soon dashed; all the time the weather was deteriorating. The morning dragged on, with no sign of their return and the wind increasing all the time, bringing up a raging sea in which neither of the two boats could be expected to live.

It was just after noon that the *Swallow* started to drag, drifting astern into deep water with the anchor off the bottom and the cable up and down, all 200 fathoms of it. The wind was now coming in furious gusts, whirling the spindrift mast high with such strength that there was no chance of the crew hoisting the smallest scrap of sail to bring the ship under control. She was rolling heavily in the rising sea, but in spite of this, the topgallant masts and yards were sent down and the sprits'l yard brought in, an amazing feat of seamanship under the circumstances, but essential for her safety. Meanwhile, with great difficulty, the capstan was manned and the bower anchor hove up and stowed.

The time passed without much hope of either boat appearing, in fact in view of the state of the sea, it was to be hoped that they were sheltering somewhere in safety. And yet suddenly a boat was sighted fleeing before the storm, making for the ship. It was almost unbelievable, but there she was, the long boat, with ten men bailing for their lives to keep her afloat. Very soon she was under the *Swallow*'s lee, to be hoisted aboard at last although not without a few bumps and broken strakes before she was on the booms.[10] There were ten men on board and they had all had a pretty bad time of it, only by good fortune sighting the ship in the nick of time. The hours had been spent under the shelter of the island riding to a grapnel clear of the surf, hoping for the weather to moderate, but at last they were blown off their mooring by the gale and immediately in danger of being swamped and drowned. To save themselves they quickly dumped the cargo of firewood and kept bailing for their lives they steered for the ship.

But what of the cutter and her crew? Carteret wanted urgently to know. The answer was not reassuring. All they could say was that Lieutenant Gower had taken all the shore party aboard the cutter together with the tent and all the other gear. This left Carteret with the conclusion that with 18 men on board, the cutter was overloaded and might well have been swamped and sunk, excellent sea boat that she was. His fervent hope was that Gower would have acted prudently and landed the people ashore again to wait for a moderation in the weather and the *Swallow's* return.

By midnight the weather had eased sufficiently to order courses and topsails to be set. This done, Carteret wore ship and stood in once again for the island. It was Sunday and daylight brought further improvement with the wind backing north-westerly and by eleven in the morning had moderated sufficiently to allow the topgallant mast and yards to be sent up again. The noon position saw the *Swallow* some four or five miles from the shore closing, steadily all the time.

But still there was no sign of the cutter. "We concluded,"

---

[10] The booms is the name of the deck space between the fore and main masts where the spare spars and boats are stowed.

wrote Carteret in his Journal, "she was lost." Yet while telescopes searched the shore and hope was fading, to their joy and relief, she was spotted lying to a grapnel close under the land with people getting into her and preparing to put out to sea. Three or four miles of turbulent water lay ahead of them, but they came out, Gower in charge, 18 men in a deep loaded boat scudding before the sea under a scrap of reefed lugsail. It was a fine feat of seamanship anxiously watched by all on board the *Swallow* until the moment they arrived safely under her lee.

It was 3 o'clock that afternoon when to Carteret's relief, they clambered on board, weary but mighty glad to be back with their shipmates again and many a good yarn to spin about their hardships and perils of the last twenty-four hours. But first the cutter had to be hoisted in, the ship got under way, and when this was done they were fed, and, on their Captain's orders, given all night in their hammocks to recover.

When the full story came to be told, they had by Gower's account experienced a hard time of it as he told Carteret later, The night before, when he attempted to bring the cutter back to the *Swallow*, she nearly foundered in the storm and only by frantic bailing by all hands had they survived to bring her to the shore where they anchored her with a grapnel just outside the surf. Leaving a small party on board to tend the moorings and keep her afloat, the rest of the men swam ashore to spend a miserable night in what shelter they could find.

Next morning they looked anxiously for the ship but there was no sign of her, and as the day wore on she still did not appear. With the wildness of the weather the previous day they feared some disaster had overtaken her and that they might not see her again. Lieutenant Gower was also of this opinion, but being a young man full of enterprise he looked to the future and perhaps with the idea of keeping up his men's morale, he had them cutting down trees to make rollers to bring the cutter ashore. If the worst came to the worst, he was prepared to see he winter out on Mas Afuera and sail for Juan Fernandez in the

Spring. No doubt he told all this to his men and if this did not cheer them up, at least the work kept them busy.

All's well that ends well, the whole ship's company could say that. After ten days of arduous and at times dangerous labour, the *Swallow's* water casks had been filled, 40 tons of it according to Kerton, and now at last the true purpose of the voyage could be pursued.

Chapter V

The wind and weather which so frustrated Carteret while watering at Mas Afuera, now allowed the *Swallow* a peaceful start to her voyage across the Pacific. For the first few days the breeze, blowing persistently from the west, kept her on a northerly course, close hauled, looking for the South-East trade wind which would eventually waft her into new and uncharted waters to the west.

Since there was no immediate prospect of making westing under the existing conditions, Carteret considered calling at the little archipelago of San Felix and San Ambrosio, which in future might be useful for British ships to wood and water now that Juan Fernandez was denied them. Meanwhile, as they sailed northward there was time to catch up on repairs and maintenance which must necessarily have been neglected during the weeks of stormy weather.

Tuesday, May 26th found the *Swallow* sailing quietly along in a light breeze on a taut bowline averaging a paltry two knots by the log. She was under all plain sail except the gaff which had been sent down on deck for repairs to the boom by the carpenters, and the main topsail which was split was also sent down on deck for stitching and another one bent on in place of it. With the improvement in the weather, Carteret decided to give the ship an airing: conditions of damp reined everywhere, personal effects, bedding and sails had little chance of being aired, neither had the cables coiled below in the tiers. Nothing had been possible in this direction since January 16th, five months ago at Port Famine. To start with, spare stores and sails were brought up on deck and the spaces cleaned out before being restowed. Next Carteret turned to the crew, ordering all hammocks on deck for washing, also their clothes, and soon every halliard and gantline aloft was festooned with an array of garments which hadn't seen a wash-tub for months.

In the end the crew, if not the ship, were in good shape, the latter thoroughly cleaned fore and aft and the former inspected by Carteret at 'divisions', Lieutenant Gower being in charge of one and Simpson, the Master, having the other. Their clothes and their persons were inspected for cleanliness. He had reason to be pleased with his crew: the period off Mas Afuera had been particularly arduous, but they had done well, and at least they had been well fed with as much fresh fish of different kinds as they could eat, a change from salt junk; and as long as they had plenty of vinegar and mustard seed[11] to eat with it they were well content.

With the light winds prevailing at this time, the *Swallow* progress was disappointing: her average day's run by the 'log' was a meagre sixty miles, needing a gale of wind or at least a good fresh breeze to hurry her along. She got that later, on Sunday, May 31st, with dire consequences. On this day, Carteret, noting the increased number of seabirds around the ship, concluded that excessive leeway had set him nearer the coast of Chile than he wished. Acting on this premise, he altered course to the west, the wind having at last gone round to the south-east the day before allowing him to do this. Perhaps this was the beginning of the South East trades which he so earnestly sought, and it came as a fresh breeze, squally at times, bringing about a pleasing increase in the *Swallow's* speed. With the wind

---

[11] An issue of these two commodities appears to be an event of some importance to the crew. Kerton mentions it frequently in his log.

now right astern, the log showed that her speeed increased to five knots and during the more prolonged squalls, she even logged seven knots for two consecutive hours. The days run on this Sunday topped 123 miles according to Kerton's log.

When Carteret reached the latitude 26 S, he made an effort to find the islands of St Felix and St Ambrose, but the various positions given by previous navigators were so dubious, particularly with regard to the longitude, that he failed to sight them. In fact, had he done so and made a survey, he would have wasted his time and found them useless for the purposed he envisaged. Later navigators reported them to be no more than rocky inlets of no use for seamen. Therefore after casting around for a while without a sighting, he turned the *Swallow* westward into the Pacific steering as far south as the trade wind permitted him

The South East trade winds blew quite boisterously, giving the *Swallow* a good push in the right direction at last. All this strong wind proved too much of a strain on the rigging, and that evening at the beginning of the first watch, about 8 o'clock according to Carteret, things started to go wrong. At the time, the *Swallow* was making the best of the fair wind with the main-topmost stans'ils set and all drawing, when a squall caught the watch completely unawares: before sail could be reduced, the main yard carried away and when all the mess was cleared up it was found to be broken at the starboard yard-arm. Worse still there was no spare spar on board to replace it, neither proper gear with which to repair it, altogether a fine measure of the poverty of the ship's equipment supplied by the Chatham Dockyard. Carteret continually bemoans this in his Journal and who could blame him? Nonetheless, with his usual determination to allow nothing to determination to allow nothing to deter him from executing their Lordship's orders he consulted the carpenter and cooper set about some sort of repair to the main yard with whatever resources were available.

The next day, work commenced at daylight. The first task

being to rig tackles to hoist the cutter clear of the deck in order to make room for the main yard which was duly unslung and lowered athwartships on the bulwarks. A careful inspection showed it to be rotten in parts where the break occurred, somewhere between the truss and the outer end of the spar[12], the implication being that had any spare yardarm been supplied, it could have been spliced in place of the broken one. However, since there were none on board, something had to be devised, and it was decided to repair the break with fishes and wolding[13], a tried and true, if cumbersome method, of effecting a semi-permanent repair. It was very much a make shift job. When the 'fishes' were in place and secured with wolding and a number of bolts, in order to make an even stronger repair, the cooper produced some of his best iron hoops which were hammered in place to add further strength to it.

The following day, Wednesday, it was decided to tackle the foremast which badly needed attention: the shrouds had been tightened so often that they were stretched up to the extent that the deadeyes were now "two blocks", as sailors say, and desperately needed shortening and set up afresh. The weather was suitable for the job, the wind blowing steadily from the south-east on the *Swallow*'s port quarter. Accordingly, sail on the foremast was reduced to take the strain off the rigging while it was being fleeted, care being taken to avoid broaching to. It was now that another of the *Swallow's* quirks was revealed. Eventually, all sail was clewed up on the foremast and yet she showed no sign of broaching to, although everything was set on

---

[12] In the period during which the *Swallow* was built ,the larger spars were fashioned in three parts and bolted together consisting of the section on either side of the truss and the yardarm at each end

[13] A 'fish' is a length of good stout timber slightly concave shaped on the inside edge and convex on the other, used to strengthen a sprung mast or yard. It is secured in place by bands of tightly bound rope lashings known as 'wolding'

the main and mizzen, in fact she steered as well as ever, even when the wind veered another point. This was against all the rules of seamanship which the crew and Carteret thought strange enough in all circumstances, so unusual indeed that he made a special note of it in his Journal[14].

With the *Swallow's* spars and rigging in as best a condition as her boatswain and carpenter could achieve with the limited means available, Carteret set her prow due west along the parallel of 28°00'S, or as near to that latitude as the wind permitted. Sailing in this direction, he bore in mind that he might fall in with the land sighted by Captain Davis, the Elizabethan seaman and discoverer, in his ship the *Bachelor's Delight*. The land believed by some to be the Southern Continent considered to exist in these latitudes to make a balance with the great continents in the Northern Hemisphere.

For the first week the winds were fresh and steady from the south-east, giving the *Swallow* a good push. Could this be the trade wind they longed for? Friday June 5th, she logged 158 miles from noon to noon reaching seven knots and three fathoms when the log was streamed, covering 28 in the first watch that day. This was a better period for the crew, the steady breeze allowing them to settle into a regular routine without constant attention to the braces or frequent clewing up and setting sail as required in more tempestuous latitudes; and best of all, a seaman's sleep in his watch below was less likely to be disturbed by the call of "all hands on deck". The boatswain and his men had the opportunity to get the rigging in the best order possible and the sailmaker to patch up his sails. In the daytime, the crew

---

[14] The *Swallow's* trim, perhaps too much by the stern, may have been the cause of this, and also may have been the reason for her reluctance to tack. The correct trim could not always be achieved; the stowage of stores, water and equipment in the hold and their use on a long voyage sometimes prevented this.

were employed in drawing the yarn from old rope creating new by knotting the strands. Sunday appears to have passed in the same activities except 'for divisions' when Carteret read out the Articles of War. There is no mention of a service, but perhaps a prayer or two was said.

Monday was a bad day for the *Swallow*, plagued as she was with light and contrary winds, and the distance by log a bare twenty-nine miles. Tuesday was much the same with light NW'ly breeze and the noon to noon run only marginally improved at thirty-three miles and not always in the right direction; in fact, at nine o'clock that evening Kerton notes "taken aback and built a chapell (sic)",[15] a term which mystifies. Wednesday was much the same with contrary winds and the *Swallow* struggling to make westing close hauled with another poor run that day of fifty-eight miles and for a while it seemed as if they had absolutely lost the trade winds. The crew were employed this day shifting iron ballast from aft forward to bring the ship more by the head. A further note in the log is the first sign of friction among the crew, when John Williams, gunner's mate, was punished for striking his superior; no mention of who his superior was nor the punishment inflicted.

By Friday June 12th, the wind came away from the SE again and for the next three days progress was good, 150 miles by log on Sunday 15th, reaching her best speed that day of seven knots for three consecutive hours. By then it was blowing a strong gale with squalls and rain, and there was always the chance that they might find themselves suddenly coming upon the mythical Davis Land and on a lee shore. However, Carteret considered it worth running the risk, as he put it in his journal "although (the

---

[15] Build a chapel: a seamen's term when a ship has lost way in a light, variable breeze, and turns completely round, boxing the compass and returning to her original course.

weather) was so thick and dark, there was the only chance we had left in so long a voyage to escape perishing by certain and unavoidable death, I mean by sickness or hunger or both." The deadly threat of scurvy was always present.

So he pressed on, relying on the lookouts to give good warning in time to alter course and stand clear; but at the same time he was becoming more and more convinced that Davis Land did not exist, since the great long rolling swell from the south gave no hint of a continent in that direction. However, the number of seabirds around meant at least an island in the vicinity, which he considered might be the one discovered by Roggeveen in latitude 27° 00' south on Easter Day in 1722 and thus named Easter Island.

In the end, Easter Island was not sighted: following to the letter the orders of the Lords of the Admiralty to steer as far south as practical precluded this; the benefit of the trade winds was also lost It was now mid-winter in those latitudes with unsettled weather and contrary winds. There were some days which were favourable, allowing the *Swallow* a noon to noon run of 150 miles; yet with anything but a fair wind she again became a sluggard, 50 or 60 being the order of the day. The wear and tear on sails and running rigging required constant attention by the sailmaker and boatswain to keep them in any sort of reasonable order: sails splitting and ropes parting were frequent occurrences, and the main employment of those not needed immediately to hand, reef or steer, was the drawing of yarns; this was then used to replace worn out running gear, but being twice-laid, as seamen say, was of poor quality.

The next week was a trying time for the *Swallow* and her crew, with head winds sometimes at gale force, and her days run reduced on Sunday 21st to a paltry forty-two miles as she strove to make westing first on one tack and then on the other. At times the wind dropped away altogether, leaving her at the mercy of a heavy swell with nothing to steady her, threatening to roll the masts out of her. Friday June 26th was a particularly trying day with the wind swinging round unheralded from NNW to SW, catching her all aback: the sudden blast carried away the purchase of the main tops'l yard tye,[16] but fortunately a preventer had been rigged which saved it from serious damage.

So it continued the rest of the week, dark, gloomy weather and contrary winds. "We might reasonably have expected better," complained Carteret in his Journal. "The sun was never above the horizon more than ten hours out of the twenty-four, and we were many days without observation or even seeing the sun." It is easy to understand his disappointment: these were tropical waters, in fact the *Swallow's* latitude was no more than two degrees south of the Tropic of Cancer. About this time, Kerton notes in his log that the ship was leaking in the hold to the extent of eight inches every hour.

The first day of July brought the east wind again with an improved days run of eighty-six miles. The number of seabirds around the ship pointed to the probability of land in the vicinity and Carteret, in order to encourage greater diligence on the part of the lookouts, promised a bottle of brandy to the first person to sight land. When the excited cry came, "land on the starboard bow" the lucky man was young Midshipman Pitcairn, who was duly awarded the bottle. He also received the honour of having the island named after him. This, their first Pacific landfall, was sighted on Thursday, July 2nd in the first dog watch at a distance of fifteen leagues, which indicates remarkable eyesight on the part of the midshipman, but since the highest point on the island is 1,000ft, it could reasonably be seen from the fore-top or the fore-topgallant yard.

The *Swallow*'s course was immediately altered towards the island, but it was soon lost to view after sunset in the gathering

---

[16] The tye is the rope attached to the centre or slings of the yard by which it is hoisted and lowered

darkness. However, the wind was fair and by 2 o'clock in the graveyard watch, the distance run by the log told them that the island was close under their lee, so they wore ship round onto the port tack and stood on until daylight when once again they wore her and laid the course for the south-west corner to obtain a closer look.

By 9 a.m. that morning, Carteret hove the *Swallow* to, one mile off the south-western corner of the island in 25 fathoms. It did not impress him excessively, "scarce better than a large rock in the ocean," he wrote, "four or some five miles round." He allowed that it had plenty of trees and noted a small fresh water stream running down the cliff side, and that there was plenty of fish, also seabirds in vast numbers. It appeared to be to be uninhabited. A boat was launched but reported that there was no landing place, at least not a practical one in view of the continual surf breaking on the coast, although Carteret considered it might be possible to land in the summer season.

Kerton's opinion was more favourable. He wrote in his log that "it appeared green and pleasant, had much wood and tuns of water, the earth a pale colour...defended by rocks and big surf." He agreed that there appeared to be no landing place and that there were fish and fowl aplenty. He also noted that the water in twenty to twenty-five fathoms was so clear that they could see the bottom from the mast head. These observations did not sway Carteret. In his opinion the island had neither sheltered anchorage nor strategic value and did not warrant further investigation.

As it turned out there were two landing places on the northern coast: Fletcher Christian and his fellow mutineers found them when they settled on this lonely desert island twenty years after the *Swallow's* visit; the most important at the north-eastern end in the vicinity of what became known as Bounty Bay, where her timbers came to rest in 1790. They also found signs of previous inhabitants and that it was sufficiently fertile for a permanent settlement, with cocoa palms and other tropical fruits and an abundance of fish, as Carteret reported. It was of volcanic origin with no reef to protect it, quite unlike other islands in the rest of the archipelago beyond the horizon.

Carteret, after his cursory survey, decided to press on: having no immediate need for wood and water, he wasted no further time and bore away for more important and useful discoveries. The position he lay down for Pitcairn before leaving was 25°02'S, 133°30'W, and whereas his latitude was only slightly in error, his longitude put the island too far west by 3°14'. But as we know, neither he nor Lieutenant Gower made use of 'lunars' and in estimating longitude by 'dead reckoning', errors were bound to accumulate. The true position of the island is 25° 04'S, 130° 16'W.

The wind being favourable, Carteret set the *Swallow* on a course west by south, still attempting to follow the instructions given him by the Admiralty, which required him to steer as far south as practical. The first days run after leaving Pitcairn Island was encouraging, 156 miles by the log with the wind often reaching gale force in which, with stuns'ls alow and aloft, she frequently managed seven knots. This however was not achieved without penalty and there were frequent entries in the log of sails splitting, rigging damaged or carried away in violent squalls accompanied by rain, thunder and lightning, not at all the weather expected in these temperate latitudes: further more, the heavy swell rolling up from the Southern Ocean found the *Swallow* making a great deal of water in the hold, which as Carteret wrote in his Journal caused her to be "very crazy". Happily he was able to confirm the usefulness of the awning over the quarter-deck which not only afforded shelter from the elements but enabled empty casks to be refilled and give the crew a generous water ration. Into each caskful caught by this means the surgeon, Thomas Watson, added spirit of vitriol. This water was mixed with the crew's grog which in Carteret's opinion, accounted for their continued good health. However, in spite of this, the weekend of the 4th of July saw the first dread signs of scurvy. It was time to abandon a southerly course in search of a mythical continent; the priority now was to find some island where fresh fruit could be obtained for the crew before they all became struck down.

The wind, however, remained persistently in the west with the *Swallow* struggling to make headway on a taut bowline day after day with no let up and disappointing progress; 38 miles on Sunday, July 5th, 66 on Monday. Tuesday was better with 81, but Wednesday was worse. All day she was beset by calms and light airs with the ship boxing the compass time and time again with only a days run of 15 miles achieved. On the credit side, there was a continuous heavy swell rolling up from the south and when the sun's meridian altitude was observed that day, the result gave a position 12 miles north of the dead reckoning. Thursday brought some improvement, 90 miles that day. No land was sighted although the large number of seabirds around the ship implied land in the vicinity and in fact two islands were passed unseen just below the horizon, both part of the Tuomotu Archipelago, Morane to starboard and Fangataufa to port.

Progress continued much the same on Friday with 82 miles logged, but soon after noon on Saturday July 11th, an island was sighted from the masthead bearing S 1/2 W at a distance of seven or eight leagues. This was a new discovery which they might easily have missed since, when the hail came, it was already well abaft the beam. Carteret described it as a "small, low, flat island almost even with the water's edge," and under the circumstances, bearing in mind the *Swallow's* chronic unweatherliness, did not consider it worth spending time beating up to it, so passed it by, giving it the name 'Bishop of Osnabery' after George III's second son. This island, now known by the Polynesian name of Mururoa, might well have been worth the endeavour of investigating: it is a coral island eighteen miles in length and eight miles wide, well wooded, no doubt with coconuts and other fruit available, just what was needed to combat the scurvy which was already getting a hold on the ship. Carteret noted the latitude to be 22° south, but his longitude of 141° 52' west of Greenwich was 2° to the westward in error.

As Mururoa faded astern, the wind veered steadily south-easterly, and thus favoured, Carteret set the course due west. The *Swallow* was now in the vicinity where in 1605, Pedro Fernandez de Quiros saw land he maintained was the much sought after Southern Continent. There followed two modest days run by the log of 108 and 131 miles, the latter being on Sunday, July 12th, when land was sighted ahead some five or six leagues distant. But this was no continent as Quiros and others maintained but only another island.

By five bells in the afternoon watch the island, known later by its Polynesian name of Nukutipipi, was close under the *Swallow's* lee. A careful study of the topography showed it to be a flat island not much above sea level some four or five miles in length, its shape being that of a half moon containing within its crescent a sheltered lagoon protected on the south-east side by a reef of red coral. It appeared to be a promising landfall, well wooded, green and pleasant where fresh food and water might be obtained. Accordingly, with this in mind, Carteret bore away to the north-west looking for a suitable anchorage. However, in spite of keeping the lead going all the time no bottom was found, so he ordered the *Swallow* to be hove to with the fore-topsail to the mast while the cutter was launched and dispatched to find a landing place.

The cutter had not long been away when a hail from the masthead told all hands that another island had been sighted to the west. Soon after this, the cutter returned to report no landing place on the island and neither water nor fruit to be seen. This was a real disappointment but there were tropic birds in great numbers, some which Kerton likened to woodcocks and so tame they were easily caught and brought aboard for the cook-pot.

About this time, Carteret was becoming increasingly anxious about the health of his crew. There was now a very urgent need for fresh food and since none was to be provided by this island, he must consider the wisdom of continuing on his present course. So far each landfall since leaving Mas Afuera had been uninhabited and yielded nothing in the way of refreshment: how many similar islands lay ahead? The *Swallow* was by now halfway across the Pacific Ocean, giving Carteret three choices: to press on in the high latitudes as instructed by their Lordships in search of the Great Southern Continent; turn the *Swallow* round and retrace his steps to Mas Afuera, recuperate his men and return home having failed, or steer a north-westerly course like most explorers had done in the past towards more fertile and rewarding discoveries, ending up in the Spice Islands where the Dutch held sway. There the crew could recuperate and the ship be repaired for the long journey home around the Cape of Good Hope.

The first of these considerations was fraught with peril due to the unseaworthiness of the ship, and now the very real danger of the crew being decimated by scurvy. The second was unthinkable being an admission of failure which was completely against Carteret's nature, while the third was the most sensible following the course of both Byron and Wallace and offering a reasonable chance of completing the circumnavigation while making further useful discoveries on the way. A decision either way had to be made soon, of that there was no doubt, but for the present there was another island to be reconnoitred, and as the wind was fair, the course was immediately set for it.

This island, later known by its Polynesian name of Andanurunga, proved as unproductive as the previous islands and was passed by, as was Anuanuaro, the next one. Carteret laid down the position of this archipelago which he named after the Duke of Gloucester, as lying in latitude 20° 30' south and longitude 146° 35' west of Greenwich, and whereas the latitude was correct the longitude was already too far west by three degrees.

But now the wind favoured Carteret, and being from the NE, the spectre of scurvy was thrust aside for a while, and the course set in a southerly direction in the hope of establishing some sign of the continent which geographers were convinced existed down there. No ship had ventured this far south into the Pacific, that vast barren, stormy expanse of ocean, the lonely domain of the whale and the albatross.

Noon the following day, Tuesday July 14th, found the *Swallow* steering WSW with a fresh breeze on her starboard quarter making a steady 5 1/2 knots, hour after hour, with stuns'ls set alow and aloft. Wednesday morning brought squalls and thundery weather, but still she ran on at a steady 5 knots although now under reduced sail. During the frequent squalls enough rainwater was caught, so Kerton records, to fill two hogsheads and five barrels.

Thursday, July 16th was a particularly trying day with squally weather from the NW and plenty of rain with it. At one bell in the first dog-watch, the topgallants had to be furled, and soon after this the wind increased further until the courses also had to be furled and the tops'ls close reefed. With the wind boxing the compass, the weary crew wore ship twice that night, once in the second dog-watch and again at 11 p.m., while the rain lashed down in heavy thunderstorms. The days run was only 56 miles.

Next day in the graveyard watch the wind dropped away to a calm; in fact by breakfast time, it was so quiet the longboat was launched and the crew turned to scrubbing the old ship's sides between the wind and water line.

On this day, Friday 17th, the *Swallow* had reached 21° 07'S, 147° 44'W according to Carteret's observations (the furthest south in that part of the Pacific of any previous explorer), when there was perceived a noticeable decrease in the great southerly swell which she had been breasting so doggedly. This lead to the speculation that this change might indicate land, an island perhaps or even a continent, and yet on the other hand it may have been due merely to a change in the weather pattern in that direction. At any rate, after a few hours, the swell returned and the direction of the wind prevented any further investigation. Soon after this it veered south-westerly and Carteret set the *Swallow*'s course northward.

The fact of the matter was that scurvy among the crew was becoming more prevalent, and so at last it had become prudent, in fact there was no alternative but to bear away to the north-west hopefully for some fertile islands where refreshment might be found which was so urgently needed. But the *Swallow* and her crew had a long way to go to achieve this.

Chapter VI

The waters into which the *Swallow*'s course now directed her proved to be the most barren stretch of ocean that her Captain could have chosen. Day after day the sun rose on an empty horizon with nothing for the lookout at the masthead to report until it set. It is true that the course made good was primarily governed by the direction of the wind, yet a couple of points to the west might have brought the *Swallow* and her crew to the Samoan Archipelago, while to the north lay Tahiti where Wallis and the crew of the *Dolphin* were recuperating and enjoying themselves with the maidens of that paradise isle.

The wind, however, made no concession. Sunday, July 19th brought a southerly breeze which kept the *Swallow* struggling to make westing close-hauled on the port tack. In the mean time, the wear and tear on the ship's fabric continued, and this morning it was found that one of the trestle trees on the foretopmast was broken and needed attention. This required the topgallant mast and yard to be struck down on deck and the topmast as well. Accordingly, after breakfast, this was done and John Renshaw, the trusty ship's carpenter, and his mates set to work repairing it, and before noon the job was done, the masts and yards swayed up and the sails set and drawing with nothing more than a slight reduction in the ship's speed. This was only a modest 88 miles from noon to noon, but the wind was steady, the longed for trade wind at last, and from now on the *Swallow's* speed picked up remarkably.

Thus on Monday, July 20th, the *Swallow*'s crew could feel with some satisfaction that they had at last the full benefit of the south-east trades. They blew steadily hour after hour wafting them along with every sail; topgallants, royals and stuns'ls all abroad and drawing to the best. 136 miles by the log was the order of the day; under such conditions they could hope for a certain relaxation with minimum attention to the sails, and best of all a four hour watch below undisturbed by the call of "all hands on deck!" It was also a good opportunity to catch up on the ship's maintenance. The carpenter and his assistants repaired and painted the boats; the sailmaker and his mates busied themselves with repairs and with stitching a new staysail; the topmen checked and maintained the rigging as best they could and the rest of the crew, when not employed in cleaning and painting the ship, were put to rousing out the cables from the tiers, giving them an airing and a chance to dry out on deck while others, when idle moments presented themselves, were put to picking oakum, a tedious but necessary job.

Wednesday was a livelier day with squalls, one of which carried away the foretopgallant stuns'ls and caused the tops'ls to be reefed. In spite of this, the distance run noon to noon was 146 miles that day. There were birds around, and a reduction in the swell suggested land to south-west, but nothing was seen. Yet islands there were; Captain Cook discovered them ten years later, an archipelago of nine altogether with surf pounding their coral reefs to become the Southern Cook Islands. But as far as water and green food were concerned, they were quite unproductive, so Carteret missed nothing there.

On Thursday, he decided to take a more northerly course in order to get into the latitude of the Solomon and Santa Cruz Islands, discovered by Mendana and Quiros in 1598 but not seen again since. Friday and Saturday were good trade wind days, particularly Saturday when the *Swallow* logged seven knots for ten hours out of the twenty-four and reached her best speed of just under eight knots when the log was streamed, the reading being seven knots and five fathoms as the sand ran out of the glass. But it was lively weather which required endless attention to the sails with constant furling and resetting. And now the wear and tear on the running rigging, halliards, sheets, lifts, braces to say nothing of clews and buntlines, was becoming a problem with the existing deficiency of spare rope to replace them. A particular shortage at this time was logline, with nothing of that sort left in the bosun's store. However, there was some untarred rope, which when picked into oakum could be spun into yarns if suitably combed. But there were no combs on board. By good fortune, it so happened that one of the seamen, a quartermaster, had some knowledge of combing the oakum to render it smooth enough to spin, and accordingly, combs were fashioned by filing nails to a fine point with which to do it. Also a machine was made by the carpenter to twist the yarn into cordage suitable for different needs.

Saturday evening brought squally weather and more wear on the running gear. Kerton noted, "cary'd away maintopmast stays'l halliards, haul'd down sail and shipped halliards end for end." Soon after this the fore top mast stuns'ls carried away as the wind freshened, so the masts were stripped down to double reefed tops'ls only. The *Swallow* was now approaching the Danger Islands, familiar to Carteret from his voyage with Commodore Byron and if he had wished to see them again, unknown to him he was in fact too far west by some three of longitude to do so. But the signs were there, seabirds in large numbers as Kerton noted in his log.

Up to this weekend stocks of water had caused no particular concern: the quantity issued twice daily to the crew was sufficient for each man's needs; and if a seaman required more, he only had to ask the officer on watch to be permitted to help himself from the scuttle-butt kept on the quarter-deck. This free and easy way was disrupted by two men caught helping themselves without leave and prompted Carteret to put all hands on a ration of one quart per day.

Water, perhaps the most important commodity on board, was not to be misused in such a way, so as to bring this home to the crew he decided on Sunday morning to make an example of the culprits. After breakfast, it being Sunday, all hands were mustered to hear Carteret read out the 'Articles of War', and when this was done, the two culprits, Richard Bransfield, seaman and James Shaunessy of the Marines were in turn lashed to a grating and each given twelve strokes of the 'cat'.

That day, the *Swallow* had a good day's run of 146 miles from noon to noon. It was a day when Carteret's ephemeris[17] told him that there was a partial eclipse of the sun, but although he hoped to see it the clouds obscured the sun much of the time and he was unable to do so. He had put the ship on a westerly course, but unbeknown to him, the Samoan Archipelago, so far undiscovered, lay on his port hand, some twenty miles distant, lush fertile islands with everything he could wish for to bring the crew back to health; yams, breadfruit and bananas to mention a few. Food itself, at this time, presented no problem as far as quantity was concerned. Wallis, it will be remembered, ordered the crews of both ships to be put on three-quarters rations, except grog. But this was way back in the Straits of Magellan and no mention was made of resuming the full amount at any time. Even so, with three-quarter ration, each member of the crew, this day being Sunday, could expect 3/4 lb of salt pork and a similar weight of biscuits for his first course followed by a good helping of ship's 'duff' for his pudding.

---

[17] Ephemeris: a table of the calculated positions of a celestial object at regular intervals throughout a period.

Next day, Monday, July 27th at noon, having reached latitude 10° 00'S, longitude 167° 00'W, and now being in the latitude of the Solomon Isles and Santa Cruz, Carteret altered course to the west intending to sail along the parallel until he sighted them.

It was to take the *Swallow* eighteen days to cover the next 1,500 miles before any land was sighted. She started the week well, day after day ploughing on with the fresh trade wind giving her a good push and a fine run of 157 miles on the Monday, and 128 on Tuesday. She followed this with five consecutive days run of 117, 114, 130, 109 and 91 miles on Sunday, August 2nd. But this headlong rush was not achieved without sails being split, stuns' l booms broken, and a fractured chainplate on the main shrouds. And now, with so much of the stores used, the *Swallow* required trimming by the stern so some of the crew, when not tending the sails, were sent below filling empty casks with sea water and stowing them at the after end of the hold while others were put to shifting iron ballast from the coal-hole[18] and restowing it in the bread-room. Sunday it may have been, but there was no rest for the crew, all hands being too busy to take any particular note of the day, but any member of the crew keeping a log or diary may have noticed that the *Swallow* was nearing the 180th meridian, half way round the globe, exactly one year since they set sail from Chatham.

The following week's run was equally good when the *Swallow* covered 876 miles by the log, and now she was sailing through the waters where, if Green's chart was correct, Carteret might expect to see the Solomon Isles or Santa Cruz. It was Monday, August 3rd with the *Swallow's* position 10° 18'S, 177° 30'W, and although he had followed the chart as diligently as he could, there was still no sign of them. He admitted in his Journal

---

[18] The coal-hole does not appear on the *Swallow's* plan, but it might be assumed to be forward under the galley.

76

that he might have passed them during some rainy weather, but he considered that it might be reasonably conjectured "there are no such islands, at least not where they are said to be laid down on our sea charts". This view was reinforced by the fact that on his voyage with Byron on the *Dolphin*, they searched for them without success. The day's run this Monday was only 69 miles.

The next day was worse with a mere 39 miles. The winds were light but a great rolling swell from the SE gave a better run on Wednesday the 5th, of 82 with the *Swallow* jogging along at three or four knots. A *Dolphin* was caught that day so the cooks made a broth of the flesh which was given to those members of the crew sick with scurvy. On Thursday, with the *Swallow's* speed picking up, as well as *Dolphin*s there were porpoises around and also albacore which often play around the bow of a ship and were harpooned by the seamen from the bowsprit to be later shared out among the crew, porpoise for the able, albacore for the sick. Friday was another day with no sight of land: the heavy swell from the SE which helped the *Swallow* on to a run that day of 96 miles gradually went round to the south, and the following day, when the breeze dropped, she fell to rolling her gunwales under with nothing to steady her. This put a great strain on her masts and rigging.

Sunday, August 9th was a day of light winds and calms with the ship's head all over the compass, sometimes boxing it and very little progress made in the right direction. In the evening there were birds around; sheerwaters, frigate birds, tropical birds and terns giving a hint of land in the offing, and one in particular, a black web-footed bird, caught and cleaned for the pot had sand and grass in its craw which seemed to confirm this. And, with the ship lying idle in the water, sharks came cruising around, the first that anyone had seen since Mas Afuera, and soon the hooks were out, baited with salt meat, catching three that day which altogether weighed 212 lbs, to be duly cooked and served to all hands and much appreciated. Next day another was caught. But still no land!

Monday brought more wind and improved sailing, but excessive rolling in the southerly swell found further weak spots in the rigging, parting one of the main topgallant shrouds. This required the sail to be quickly furled and the mast struck while the shroud was spliced and set up again. This done, the mast and yard were soon swayed up and the sail set, all in the day's work.

At this stage the leak which Kerton noted in his log had increased and was giving cause for concern. This was nothing unusual in an old ship. Leaks would anyway tend to increase in boisterous weather. But a free surface of water slopping about in the hold might affect the stability and trim, and if the pumps were not to be kept going all the time, the leak must be stopped. Eventually it was found in the gunner's store, right in the eyes of the ship where the strakes were secured to the stem. One of them had sprung just below the waterline and repairs would have to wait until the ship came to anchor in a sheltered mooring.

By now scurvy was getting a serious hold on the crew, while Carteret himself was suffering a severe stomach disorder and it was only with a great effort of willpower that he was able to keep the deck. The need for a tropical island and anchorage to recuperate the crew and repair the ship was now vital.

On Tuesday a number of logs were seen drifting by, raising the hope of all hands that land indeed was in the vicinity.

At last, one blessed day, just as dawn was breaking, the longed for hail of land in sight was heard from the masthead. It was 5.15 a.m. on Wednesday, August 12th, 79 days since they took their departure from Mas Afuera. The land, or island, since as yet it was uncertain which, bore WSW eight or nine leagues distant, so without further ado the sails were trimmed and the *Swallow* hauled her wind to the south on a course directly for it.

The trade wind was fresh this morning with the ship making a good six knots when the log was streamed, and soon it became apparent that it was an island. Not long after, another was sighted bearing South by West, a distance of ten leagues, and there were more to come. By six bells there were altogether seven islands in sight in just about all quarters of the compass, one in particular seen from the masthead bearing NW, Kerton described in his log as "high peaked, like a sugar loaf, which smoked and appeared to be volcanic". Carteret, mighty relieved at last to be on the verge of discovery, named the archipelago the "Charlotte Isles," after King George III's Queen. Kerton reckoned the position of the first island to be sighted was in Latitude 10° 40' South, Longitude 163° 30' East of London. The latitude was good but with regard to the meridian, the estimate was 2° 30' too far west.

Carteret did not know at this time that this sighting was not a new discovery, but was in fact seen by Mendana and Queros in 1595 and mistakenly charted 1,500 miles further east. At the time it was given the name 'Santa Cruz', the very island Carteret had searched for way back in July. However, not knowing this he named it after Lord Egmont, while the other large island to the south became Lord Howe Island.

The breeze continued fresh and fair and by breakfast time the *Swallow* had reached a position close in to the eastern end of the island. Sail was shortened and the course altered northward. The shore was low-lying and fringed with mangroves, but inland it was green and pleasant with hills rising to three or four hundred feet. It appeared to be inhabited since about this time smoke was seen on the NE part of the island. By 9.15 a.m. the north-eastern extremity was abeam and the coast opened up with a promise of sheltered bays where a suitable anchorage might be found. After clearing the point, which Carteret named Cape Byron, the cutter, under the command of Simpson, was sent to investigate. He returned at eleven to report the unsuitability of the bay, having obtained sounding indicating a rocky bottom of hard coral. The next bay was more promising and he was able to signal that a suitable berth had been found.

On the receipt of this, sail was made, but the *Swallow* was unable to fetch the anchorage, so the helm was put down to bring her on the other tack. However, she would not have it, although she was in smooth water. In the end they had to wear her. Neither would she oblige them next time, nor the time after, being in one of her moods, nor was it until several boards later at 3.30 p.m. that they were able to drop the best bower on a bottom of fine sand and mud, veering out two thirds of the cable to hold her. Then, while the cutter went off again looking for water, the crew, anticipating a few days at anchor, snugged the ship down by striking the topgallant and spritsail topsail yards down on deck. At eight bells in the first dog watch the cutter returned, and Simpson was able to report that he had found an excellent watering place close by the anchorage. He also had some further good news; he was able to confirm that the island was inhabited having encountered two natives who appeared as the cutter approached the shore, but did not stay; and after making some unwelcoming signs, retired into the forest. He noted that they were armed with bows and arrows. But now it was getting dark and any further exploration must wait until next day.

That evening, as Carteret studied the island from the anchorage, he was of the opinion that, from its appearance, their prospects for the immediate future were looking brighter. Here at last there might be peace and a fair chance of rest for all hands, an opportunity to bring the *Swallow* by the stern to repair the leak, and the expectation of obtaining fresh food for the invalids. The island was covered with trees which came right down to the sea, mangroves by the shore, but beyond them in the interior were pandana and banyan trees, and certainly coconut for the taking, if they could be got at conveniently. Furthermore, there were natives on the island who might be willing to trade, with the possibility of obtaining fruit and livestock.

The hope was there, also the determination to succeed, but the good fortune which had favoured the *Swallow* and her crew across the Pacific, now appeared to desert them.

Chapter VII

Although anchored close inshore, the roadstead, later known as *Swallow* Bay, had no great depth in contour, thus offering very little in the way of shelter from the brisk trade wind blowing from the east. The swell which it brought in caused the ship to roll uneasily at her moorings, and if the problem with the leak was to be properly addressed, a quieter anchorage had to be found. On the following day, Thursday, August 14th with this in mind, Carteret ordered the cutter to be launched and made ready to embark on a survey of the coast to seek a better one. Simpson, the master, was to be in charge of the cutter, with a complement of fifteen seamen to man her.

In the mean time, it was Lieutenant Gower's task to take the longboat ashore for water and, having seen the casks loaded, he set off with six men for the watering place. Those of the *Swallow*'s crew not engaged in boatwork were employed in setting up the fore topgallant rigging; others were kept busy shifting stores aft to bring the *Swallow* by the stern to allow the carpenter to get at the leak in the bow.

At this juncture, Carteret was becoming increasingly ill with a severe stomach complaint, in fact much of the running of the ship devolved on Lieutenant Gower's shoulders, hence his reason for sending Simpson away in the cutter to carry out surveying while keeping Gower at hand to take over command if the situation required. He could rely on Gower who, throughout the voyage had shown himself to be a reliant and competent seaman. Simpson unfortunately, although an equally competent seaman, was less reliable as events later proved.

Carteret's instructions to Simpson were clear. The primary purpose of the expedition, he told him, was to find a more suitable anchorage, but while doing so, no risks were to be taken and to be always on his guard. Friendly relations were to be encouraged with the islanders and at the same time, care must be taken not to give umbrage. Furthermore, in no case should he leave the boat nor allow more than two men to do so for any purpose. If threatened by a number of canoes, he was to return to the ship, but if he was in no danger from them, he might endeavour to cultivate their friendship by civil and cordial behaviour and the offer of a few beads and other trifling things. In the event of any man going ashore, the rest of the crew must stand to arms ready for defence. Nothing was to divert him from finding a new anchorage and to return to the ship as soon as possible.

A change of routine was always welcome to the seamen, especially where there was the opportunity of a run ashore, and they were in no doubt all in good heart with the prospect of adventures similar to those experienced at Mas Afuera. Even Simpson appeared to share their feeling, for in the joy of his independent command, he paid scant regard for his captain's orders, in fact for the most part he ignored them. But this was no jaunt: the natives of these islands were savages and might even be cannibals so, in case they should prove to be hostile, each man was issued with a musket or blunderbuss together with powder and shot. It was a fine day as the cutter set off; her crew, which included Midshipman Pitcairn, hoisted the sails and Simpson set the course to the west, investigating any likely bay or inlet while taking soundings where possible.

Meanwhile, back at Swallow Bay, Lieutenant Gower was having difficulty in getting water. Kerton was one of the boat's crew, and his account tells us that prior to the boat leaving for the watery place, some of the islanders had been seen making signs of welcome and encouragement to come ashore. When at last Gower reached the watering place he could see that they were well armed with bows, arrows and spears, so as a gesture he ordered his men lay down their muskets, and it appeared that the islanders did the same with their boys. Now was the opportunity to talk with them, to make friends, and with this mind he stepped ashore, watched assiduously by those on board the *Swallow*.

Gower had not proceeded far when the islander's treachery was revealed as arrows began to fall, causing him to retreat hurriedly to the boat where three of the seamen let off their muskets. Whether fired in a moment of panic or not it sent the islanders scurrying back into the words. None of the arrows had hit the boats crew. After this, the seamen landing and watering commenced for a time without further harassment.

While the watering was going on, Simpson sailed to the westward in search of a better anchorage. Skirting the coast, he looked into two bays, neither of which was suitable, then sailed onward altogether a distance of about 14 miles when a village was sighted on the north east part of the island which appeared interesting enough to investigate further. As the approached, several neat, cane built palm leaf covered houses were seen, and there were canoes drawn up on the beach, small narrow ones with outriggers, each with room for two, perhaps three men. These were coconuts and other fruit trees nearby and more in the woods beyond. As for inhabitants, few could be seen, five or six only, but no women or children; the villagers watched the cutter come in without any opposition.

Disregarding his Captain's specific orders Simpson landed, and taking a few men with him, approached the natives, who appeared apprehensive but stood their ground. These might be elders or chiefs; sturdy well built men, quite black with woolly hair, some having bones piecing their noses and looking fierce.

However, after some friendly gestures from Simpson, they led the seamen to a structure, probably the village canoe house, and perhaps used by the natives as a meeting place. Here, by signs, Simpson tried to make his wants understood which he did with singular success, and with the helps of a few beads he brought quite a generous response of coconuts, bananas and plantains, also boiled fish and yams. There was a fruit tree nearby, which Kerton was later informed resembled custard apples, but they would let them have none of them. They appeared to have plenty of fish by all the nets of different sizes, drying out on the canoes, although none so far had been caught.

It was time to return to the ship. A more suitable anchorage had not yet been found, but contact with the islanders had been established and amenable relations formed. So far, so good, but Simpson had hoped to obtain a greater quantity of fruit, and here at hand were trees with coconuts galore. Why not cut one down? Then they could fill the boat with nuts and also cut off the young shoots, so green and tender, to be cooked and given to those back on the ship suffering from scurvy. So giving the order, this was immediately done.

It was a stupid, thoughtless, deed fraught with disastrous consequences for the *Swallow* and her crew. A growing tree to the islanders was an essential source of food. Chopped down it was nothing. It would also be somebody's property and might even have a 'tabu' on it. The attitude of the elders changed immediately, protesting, perhaps threatening. In return, with the obvious intention of impressing them with his superiority, Simpson drew his pistol, aimed at a mark and fired.

This made little if any impact. The islanders at that moment were gathering by the houses, armed and ready to attack with Simpson taking scant notice until midshipman Pitcairn drew his attention to the danger. At last, when it was almost too late, he gave the order to get aboard the cutter and pull clear.

In fact, for some of the crew, it was too late. The arrows were beginning to fly, some already finding a mark, while out in the bay a host of canoes was gathering. Soon they were under attack from sea and shore, and while those at the oars pulled for their lives, the others opened fire on their pursuers, who followed them into the water as far as they could, still shooting their arrows in deadly earnest.

The danger now threatened from the canoes, their arrows beginning to rain down on the cutter, while in return the seamen fired their muskets and blunderbusses in ragged volleys, the blunderbusses in particular wounding many and killing others, each being loaded with eight or more pistol bullets. Yet they came on undeterred, paddling as fast as they could to cut them off, twenty or more canoes, their occupants shooting their arrows in deadly earnest, quite undaunted by the musket fire.

It was a near thing; at last they were able to pull clear of their pursuers, but it was not achieved without several of the crew being wounded, Simpson himself being struck by three arrows. Midshipman Rowe was also wounded and five of the seamen, with serious consequences.

It was a sorry crew which returned to the *Swallow* coming aboard having been away all day with nothing achieved save bringing back seven wounded men.

The Master's report, as given to Carteret, was a deep disappointment. When apprised of the whole story, he was justifiably angry with Simpson for disobeying his orders so flagrantly. What reprimand he gave him is not recorded, but his displeasure comes out in his Journal, laying the blame squarely on his shoulders for the subsequent failure of the voyage.[19] Simpson, any way, was now a sick man, as were the other wounded men; Samuel Smith, seaman and James Fogarty of the Marines, being the most serious. There was particular concern for the casualties as it was feared that the arrows might be poisoned.

Saturday was a breezy day with the trade wind blowing into the bay from the north-west. The shore in the way of the watering place was steep, and with the sea breaking against it made it, too risky for the boats to land a party. But there were other matters to attend to; the leak in the bow which had the attention of John Renshaw, the carpenter and his mates, while those seamen fit enough were put to work setting up the fore and main catharpings and shrouds. The number of seamen available for the rigging was sadly reduced by scurvy and yesterday's wounds, and now the gunner, an important man on any warship who normally had charge of a watch, was confined to his cabin with scurvy.

By noon the wind was really piping, swinging the *Swallow* round until she rode with her stern uncomfortably near the shore. At 2 p.m. the situation was worse, the cutter and longboat were hoisted in and the small bower anchor let go. Then, to ease things further, the topgallant yards and masts were sent down. But the anchors with a good scope of cable held her fast. It was disturbing however, to see a large number of islanders gathering, clearly visible amongst the trees, an ever-present threat preventing any attempt to get water.

---

[19] On the day Carteret beheld the island "so agreeable in appearance" as he put it, he considered his travails at an end. "But," he wrote, "those were only delusions which served to make the disappointment greater and all my fine hopes of further success vanished by the ill behaviour of Mr Simpson, the Master."

Next day, Sunday April 16th, weather conditions were more favourable. The wind had veered round to the SSE and was blowing moderately. The islanders were still there, and now Carteret decided that firm steps must be taken if they were ever going to get water, a salutary lesson was needed since any friendly relationship was out of the question. Launching the cutter and longboat, one was sent to the watering place with a cable and stream anchor, while the other was directed to take a hawser from the *Swallow's* starboard quarter to be, as Kerton wrote in his log, 'clap'd on the best bower' and used as a spring when the time came.

While the boats were attending to the moorings, the *Swallow's* port-lids were raised on the larboard side and the guns run out which together with the swivels were all loaded with grapeshot. This done, the cable on the best bower was layed out; then a check on the spring brought the larboard broadside in full view, half a cable from the shore while the islanders watched, quite unimpressed and unaware of the threat.

The roar and the blast of shot from the first broadside, six-pounders only, but frightening to the uninitiated, cleared the foreshore, killing and wounding some of them while others fled into the woods beyond. This was the time for the longboat, piled high with empty barrels, to make for the watering place, with the cutter well-manned and well-armed to give them covering fire. The bank was steep where they landed and for a quarter of an hour they were able to carry out their task unseen until the islanders, gathering their wits after the shock of the broadside, went on the attack again. They lacked nothing in bravery, showing the same determination experienced by Simpson on the previous day; in fact some of them may have been amongst those involved in yesterday's attack on the cutter, having followed her as she made her way along the coast back to the *Swallow*.

Soon the arrows began to fall among the longboat's crew wounding seaman Joseph Cawsey in his belly, while

Midshipman Pitcairn had a narrow escape when an arrow struck the barrel he waas sitting on, with such force as to penetrate right through a stave. This emphatically demonstrated the power of the islander's bows, each of seven feet, with five foot long arrows with a bone tip. In return, the cutter's crew fired volley after volley with their muskets, but this did little to deter them from crawling on their bellies from the wood to get within range of the watering party.

Clearly, this could not be allowed to continue. Valuable lives would be lost. Another lesson was needed to permit the watering to go on. Accordingly, the guns were run out again and the swivels prepared. In the meantime, a signal was made to the boats to return to the ship.

All was ready for another broadside. The seven six pounders and swivels, loaded with grape, tore into the wood, killing and wounding many of the islanders hiding there, while those able to do so escaped, some two hundred of them, fleeing along the shore to gather at the western point where they appeared confident that they were safely out of range. In this they were mistaken, not yet realising the power of a cannon, and on Carteret's orders a six pounder was aimed at them, and when fired the ball fell short, but skimming along the shallow water ploughed into their midst. This was too much for them. They fled, leaving the *Swallow's* crew free to continue the watering without further interference. But even so, to discourage any further attempts to disrupt the proceedings inremittent gunfire was directed into the woods until the boats returned with their load of casks.

Although not all the butts were filled the quantity of water on board was deemed sufficient for the time being, and not worth risking any further confrontation with the islanders. Time to leave this inhospitable bay and seek new pastures, better anchorages where more friendly islanders might be contacted. Accordingly the boats were hoisted in, the topgallant masts sent up and the after spring cleared from the best bower, all ready to get under way at first light.

While preparations to sail were being made Carteret, now so badly afflicted by the stomach disorder, was forced to retire to his bed. It was time to take stock of the present situation, bearing in mind the parlous state of the ship and her crew, whether to pursue further exploration or abandon the voyage and return home by one route or another. In his present condition he considered that he was unlikely to survive much longer and if he should die, he must be certain that Lieutenant Gower, as second in command, was aware of the best course to pursue. With this in mind he sent for him, together with Simpson the Master, to take part in the discussion. These two men, both seasoned circumnavigators, were very different in character: Gower, a Welshman with a background of privilege, a commissioned officer and fine seaman well thought of by Carteret; Simpson, a Scot by all accounts but only a warrant officer, an obstinate and uncompromising man who showed this by his disregard of specific orders the day before. Carteret also had some doubt as to his ability as a navigator. There, in the Great Cabin, they discussed the situation. The wide stern window gave them a fine view of the bay, the scene of such execution among the islanders, where according to reports, the groans and cries of the wounded and dying could still be heard in the woods beyond. Swallow Bay marked the low point of the voyage where Carteret's hopes and expectations were brought to nought.

To start with, he outlined the future course the voyage might take if they were to satisfy the Lords of the Admiralty in London. Having procured provisions, refreshed the crew, cleaned and repaired the *Swallow* as best they could, and then, if the condition of crew and ship proved satisfactory, they might pursue the following course. Firstly, they would continue westward until they reached the mainland which he imagined lay not far ahead. Then, with the southern summer coming on and the winds favouring them, the *Swallow* would bear away south in as high a latitude as possible in search of the Great Southern

Continent. Having done this, if circumstances permitted, to return home, either westward towards the Cape of Good Hope, or eastward to the Falkland Islands and thence home to England.

Having told them all this, he laid out his charts to show them their present position, and put it to them that, should they desire to pursue the voyage, the decision must be theirs in the event that he might succumb to his illness. They must bear in mind the condition of the ship, her unhandiness, the leak and her unsheathed bottom already so foul and perhaps worm-eaten. Furthermore, the quantity of stores remaining on board was inadequate for an extended time at sea without a severe reduction in rations for all hands.

He then gave the two men the alternative course. If the true purpose for the voyage were to be abandoned, the *Swallow*'s bows must be turned northwards towards one of the European settlements in the East Indies where the crew might be refreshed, the ship repaired and restocked for the homeward voyage. If this was to be their decision, he told them that it must be taken at the earliest opportunity in order to make use of the South-West Monsoon while it lasted.

After mature consideration both Lieutenant and Master were in agreement that, in the best interests of the ship and crew it would be advisable to abandon further exploration. The most prudent course was to haul to the north directly with the Monsoon favouring them at present, and seek repairs to the ship and refreshment for the crew at Batavia or some convenient port. They did not believe that anything was to be gained in further contact with the islanders without running risk of incurring casualties in either officers or men, since scurvy and wounds had left the ship gravely short-handed as it was. "In consequence," wrote Carteret in his Journal, "on finding that they both shared his sentiments, I gave orders to the Lieutenant to weigh (at) the first opportunity he could." However, he was reluctant to leave the island without one last attempt to find a safe haven, and he included in his orders that the course should be directed along the coast on the north side of the island where a suitable anchorage might be found.

Monday morning opened with squally weather and heavy rain. At 6 a.m. all hands were turned out to weigh anchor and make sail. With Lieutenant Gower in command the course was set to take the *Swallow* out of the Bay and thence westward, keeping a distance of one mile off the shore. By five bells she was under topgallants, making four knots with leadsmen in the chains sounding at intervals but no bottom at 40 fathoms. The shore was inviting, so green and fertile, with coconuts and other fruit trees near the water's edge, and several bays were passed which could have made suitable havens, but for the hostile islanders lurking there. Carlisle and Byron Bays were the names chosen for two of them.

Later in the watch the wind became light and variable with the *Swallow* making slow progress. By 10 a.m. she had reached a position abreast of 'Bloody Bay', the scene of Simpson's disastrous encounter and by noon, having covered fourteen miles, the trend of the coast opened up a headland which bears the name of Carteret Point. There were villages clearly visible on the shore, each one laid out in an orderly fashion with dwellings which Kerton described as being 'like small country houses in England', a touch of nostalgia perhaps, and he noted that some of them appeared to be stone built with thatched roofs. The villages also had defensive walls of stone held together with a mortar of some kind or so it seemed. They possessed plenty of livestock, large hogs and poultry also, but on the *Swallow's* approach to a village, all women, children and livestock were led away to safety in the jungle beyond.

It was now close on noon: time to get the octants out to determine the latitude by the sun's meridian altitude, which having been measured, gave their latitude as 10° 42' South. Kerton recorded this in his log, but made no mention of the longitude. But with regard to his latitude, he was a little at fault in his calculation which on a present day chart would have put him squarely in the jungle beyond the northern shore.

Soon after noon, the *Swallow* cleared Carteret Point; a fine, sheltered bay or lagoon opened out about 1 1/2 miles wide, and as viewed from the masthead some six miles in length. As an anchorage it was inviting, but no order was given to enter, a wise decision with regard to the *Swallow*'s unhandiness in confined waters, and neither was the cutter sent in, although under more favourable conditions it might have turned out to be a very fine anchorage, if friendly relations with the islanders could have been established. By 1 o'clock they were off Cape Trevanion, the extreme north-western end of the land where the *Swallow* hauled her wind on a southerly course maintaining a distance of half a mile from the shore while the cutter looked into every bay and inlet.

The main feature of the coastal scene was dense tropical jungle with villages on the fringe which supported a population in fishing as seen by the number of canoes drawn up on the beaches, some small ones for three or four men, but there were larger ones with canopies which were more likely to be sea-going rather than fishing craft, used for inter island commerce. Although Carteret had no personal contact with the islanders, from the description given him by others he recorded in his 'Journal' that they were above average stature compared to European build, of a copper colour with dark woolly hair and little beards; altogether an active, nimble people who wore no clothes and were quite at home on the water as if it were their natural element. They appeared to be governed by chiefs or headmen to whom they gave obedience. They were in fact a simple, stone-age people, well adapted to their surroundings that guarded their territory with great determination. It was soon established that the west end of the island extended seven miles to the south, with an inlet three miles down the coast which, when investigated by the cutter, turned out to be a narrow channel, only navigable by small craft, leading into the lagoon, but further exploration was denied them as a number of canoes were gathering with the intention of cutting them off.

Very soon they were running the gauntlet of the arrows, and in spite of the crew stretching out on their oars with all their might, it was touch and go until Gower fired his musket at the leading canoe. This frightened the crew enough to slow them down for a while. But other canoes came on and the situation began to look bad for the cutter and her crew until someone on board the *Swallow* saw the danger and ordered the six pounders to be run out. When at last the cutter gave them a clear shot a blast of grape was sent into the leading canoes. This caused the occupants to leap overboard in terror while others abandoned the chase. When the cutter at last came alongside she was towing an abandoned canoe, with bows and arrows still on board and also one islander who refused to abandon it, and although shot and wounded in head and arms and being beaten about unmercifully by the cutter's oars, was brought aboard where the surgeon declared he would not live. In spite of all this he seemed to recover somewhat and was allowed, on Carteret's orders, to make off with his canoe rowing away with his one good arm and great fortitude.

The departure of this man was the last contact the *Swallow* had with these intrepid islanders who, with their primitive weapons, defended their shores so successfully. And now, there was no longer anything to be gained by remaining in these waters. Egmont Island, where Carteret had entertained such high expectations, had failed him; ill health, Simpson's disobedience to his orders and a determined and hostile people had contributed to this disappointment. It was time for the *Swallow* to leave. Somewhere to the north-west lay the Solomon Islands and New Britain where fortune might look more favourably on her. Carteret, still confined to his quarters with his stomach disorder, watched Egmont Island fade into the distance with feelings of frustration, and later wrote about the islanders in his Journal that, "if I had not been ill I would have taught these people better manners to strangers!"

Chapter VIII

The second dog watch after taking her departure from Egmont Island found the *Swallow* steering WNW before a gentle trade wind which barely filled her patched and sun bleached sails. As the island, which caused Carteret so much disappointment, faded over the horizon, the log, when streamed at eight bells, showed her to be making only a meagre two knots. The canoes, those which had attacked the cutter in the afternoon were left far behind, but in the second dog watch another little fleet hove in sight making for the island. A watch was kept on them, but they appeared quite peaceful, as if returning from a fishing expedition and they passed by without taking any particular notice of the ship.

By sunset, the little sugar loaf island of Tanakula was abeam, the plume of smoke from its 2,000 ft summit clearly seen streaming away to leeward. During the night the breeze increased with squalls, thunder and lightning and by the end of the morning watch, the *Swallow's* speed had greatly increased and the log showed her to be making a good six knots. At 8 o'clock all hands were assembled to witness the punishment. Private Robert Brown, of the Royal Marines, had been caught stealing wine from the sick bay. For this, instead of the usual stoppage of grog or flogging at the grating, he was sentenced to run the gauntlet whereby, to his shame, his shipmates beat him unmercifully about the head and body as he ran down the lane between them.

The following day, Thursday, August 20th, opened with a strong easterly breeze, giving the *Swallow* a days run of 149 miles. At any time there would be another landfall, the indications were there; seabirds, man-of-war birds in particular, so Kerton wrote in his log, and sometimes the scent of the land borne by the wind. Their desire for a landfall became even greater with the passage of time and with it the urgency for refreshment for the crew, which was Carteret's greatest concern together with the ever present need for water. To be on the safe side, he ordered the ration to be reduced to one quart per day but left the grog unchanged. Meanwhile, it was discovered that sea water from the leak in the bow had entered the sail locker, which if not attended to directly would rot the canvas, so all the spare sails were roused out on deck to be hung up or draped in the sunshine to dry.

Friday morning commenced with a fresh breeze and thundery showers, but as the day wore on the weather cleared and at noon the log showed a fair days run of 120 miles. During the previous two days the course steered ran parallel to the Solomon Island of Malaita some 60 miles off, whereas a more westerly course could have brought an earlier sighting. There were charts of this coast on board, but bearing in mind the *Swallow's* unhandiness, a lee-shore was something to be wary of and given a wide berth. Carteret, still confined to his cabin, recorded his apprehensions in his Journal. "Had we got into any gulf or deep bay," he wrote, "it would have been impossible to get out with our sickly crew and bad ship." Islands in this respect were more welcome where a suitable lee could be found, although coral reefs and deep water were a problem when looking for a safe anchorage.

At 10.30 that morning, land was sighted to the westward and soon afterwards the course was altered towards it. In appearance it was green and pleasant, an island in fact. Carteret laid down its position as 7° 56'N 157° 03'W and chose to name it Gower Island[20] after the young lieutenant, a compliment which he richly deserved. At 1 p.m. the cutter was launched with Gower in command to investigate it. Meanwhile the *Swallow* lay hove to keeping a lookout for a signal that a suitable anchorage had been found, but initially the surf was too heavy in the eastern side, so Gower shaped a course round to the lee on the west, and soon after was able to signal that he had obtained soundings of 60 fathoms, but poor holding ground it being hard coral bottom.

On receiving this information Carteret, still indisposed and confined to his cabin, gave the order to find a suitable landing place in order to procure coconuts or any other fruit available, and this Gower immediately set about doing. As the cutter approached the shore, two men were seen on a rocky prominence making frantic signals for the cutter to keep away. In appearance, these natives were similar in colour and stature to those on Egmont Isle and obviously not at all welcoming by the signs they made, gestures quite frantic but as they were not threatening Gower persisted, bringing the cutter close in while making signs that all they wished for were some coconuts. At last this was understood and one of the islanders shinnied up a tree throwing down over a dozen coconuts which pitched into the water to be retrieved by the boat's crew. Soon after this Gower approached them with some small articles which interested them, and thus encouraged they pointed out the village indicating that more coconuts and other fruit might be had.

This was good news, but before any further overtures were to be made to the islanders a secure anchorage for the *Swallow* had to be found. Two more bays were investigated but failed to produce anything better, so it was decided that if the ship was

---

[20] It's present day name is Dai Island

brought close in to the shore a reasonable berth could be achieved with a good scope of cable out on the best bower.

At 4 p.m the *Swallow* steered towards the coast and into smooth water. When she was within two cables of the shore, the helm was put down to bring her to the wind and although she came round as far, at the critical point as so often happened with the 'old ship', she lost momentum, was caught in the stays, and started to drift directly onto the nearby rocks. She was only saved by a timely order which sent her crew hurrying to the braces to back the main and mizzen yards. Who gave this order at this moment of great danger is not recorded – Gower was away in the cutter, Carteret and Simpson on the sick list – but at any rate, on of the master's mates or midshipmen was alert, and with sails aback and helm hard a'weather, she made a stern board thus clearing the danger and avoiding certain destructions by the narrowest of margins.

Having failed to find an anchorage, there was nothing for it but to stand off through the night and return at daylight the following morning for the rendezvous with the islanders. After hoisting in the cutter, the *Swallow* was prepared for a night hove to under easy sail. As it turned out the wind freshened and soon she was under reefed topsails, wearing ship every hour or two in order to maintain a safe distance from the shore. After sunset the night became so black that the island was lost to view except during occasional flashes of tropical lightning.

With the passing of the hours the current set the ship well to the south west and at daylight, Gower Island was nowhere in sight, but the lookout reported a small island to the south west with another larger one beyond. These were duly charted, the smaller one being named for Simpson, the other Carteret Isle; although later this was found to be one of the southern Solomon's known as Malaita. Simpson Island now bears the name of Maana'oba Island on modern charts. Further west, a little archipelago was sighted from the masthead, the largest of which now bears the name of Ramos Isle, but too far off to investigate if the ship was to get back to Gower Island in time for the meeting with the islanders.

The breeze had fallen light by then and it was not until 10 o'clock that the *Swallow* reached the island where the natives in their canoes were waiting and soon the trading began. The canoes, each with four men in them, were full of coconuts and yams and there was particular interest from the islanders in the items Gower had for exchange, but they tried to drive a hard bargain, agreeing too much yet surrendering very little in exchange once they had obtained their desired purchases.

It was soon evident to Gower that there was little likelihood of getting the quantity of fruit which the ship so urgently needed, but in the meantime, the islanders made signs that if the cutter followed them to the shore where one or two native huts could be seen, they would trade with them there, even going as far as to hold on to the cutter while paddling their canoes shoreward. The earnestness of their efforts to persuade Gower to this end, caused him to become suspicious that they had designs on the boat and that a trap was being laid for them. He decided to return to the ship to consult Carteret.

Carteret was still indisposed and confined to his cabin, but when Gower made his report, he decided the time had come when these natives should be taught a lesson. In this respect he was abandoning his initial aim to establish friendly relations, and was now resorting to the actions which had failed so dismally on Egmont Isle and was about to follow his precept of teaching them better manners to strangers. This lesson consisted of ordering a gun to be run out and a shot fired over their heads.

At its discharge the islanders fled for their lives, paddling for the shore as fast as they could with the cutter in full pursuit. And now the spirit of the chase seemed to have taken hold of the cutter's crew, together with a desire for revenge for those shipmates dying from their wounds received at Egmont Isle. On the *Swallow*, men were loosing off their muskets at them, while

Gower was doing the same from the cutter, and already two of the natives had been hit. But try as hard as they did, pulling with all their might, the cutter could not come up with them, their sails, their paddles and the swift shape of the canoes gave them a better speed. It appeared to Gower, as the chase continued, that their intention was to lure him to the village where help was available in order to capture the cutter, but by steering a course to intercept them, he foiled their plan, forcing them further up the coast. When all the islanders reached the shore they quickly pulled their canoes onto the beach and ran for the shelter of the woods.

The cutter was not far behind them and Gower wasted no time in landing several men in order to capture the canoes. Others were directed to give covering fire to keep the islanders pinned down in the woods and discourage any retaliation with their deadly arrows. Soon the shore party were back to the cutter dragging two canoes along with them, still loaded with coconuts and yams. It was altogether a successful foray with no casualties incurred, and having acquired a quantity of much needed fruit. No time was wasted in getting back to the *Swallow* which they did, towing the canoes with them.

After unloading the canoes, one of them was cast adrift and sunk while the other was brought on board. A study of the one retained showed it to be a particularly well-made craft, no crude dug-out, but one constructed of planks, lashed to frames with fibre and the seams caulked with a black sticky substance which was considered by those on board to be superior to pitch. Altogether, quite a remarkable vessel considering these islanders were still in the Stone Age with no iron to make knives or axes and their arrows tipped only with flint or bone.

The remainder of the morning was employed by Lieutenant Gower surveying the coast, but on returning to the ship with nothing suitable found in the way of an anchorage, Carteret gave the order for the *Swallow* once again to be put on a course towards New Britain. The trade wind was brisk and progress good to start with, but as they approached the "doldrums", the breeze began to drop away and with it the *Swallow's* speed. But even then, it could bring up a squall every now and then which it did on the morning of September 22nd. Altogether, it was an unfortunate day for the *Swallow* and her crew, a Sunday as it happened, with the scurvy beginning to take hold and one man dying, while another succumbed to his wounds. And to make matters worse, a marine was lost.

At breakfast time that morning a sudden rain squall bore down on the ship which carried away the fore top-gallant studding sail boom and while the watch was putting this to rights, the stark cry of 'man overboard' was heard. Patrick Dwyer who had been working by the port quarter lost his hold and fell into the sea and with the speed the *Swallow* was making, some five or six knots at the time, Dwyer was soon left astern. As quick as they could, while the ship was being hove to, some members of the watch attempted to launch the canoe, the one captured from the islanders, being light and handy, but in their hurry, it was damaged and stove in by striking one of the guns. It immediately sank, but meanwhile the cutter was launched. However, all this took time and the marine was drowned and sank before they reached him.

The other members of the crew who died this day were James Cooper, Armourer, who succumbed to scurvy and Samuel Smith, seaman, of his wounds and the tetanus which followed. That evening, in the second dog watch, the bodies of the two men were committed to the deep with all due ceremony and soon after this was done the personal effects of the deceased were auctioned. This was done in the customary way, the would-be purchasers assembling at the mainmast to bid for them with the cost being deducted from their pay and the total remitted to the next of kin at the end of the voyage.

Monday was a day of light winds and slow progress, sixty-nine miles only by the log, but the set and drift of the current was in their favour finding the *Swallow* ten miles ahead of the observed position at noon. There were sea birds around in large numbers that evening with the likelihood of islands in the vicinity, but the weather became unsettled with squalls and rain reducing the chance of a sighting. Nonetheless, an hour before midnight, land, or at any rate the sea breaking on the shore, was seen almost abeam to larboard. But investigation had to wait until daylight and accordingly the *Swallow* was put under easy sail for the rest of the night.

Daylight revealed an interesting cluster of small islands, six in number, completely surrounded by a reef about eight miles in diameter, each one green and promising with many coconut trees in evidence. The discovery was a new one, although Carteret was unaware of this at the time since other explorers had sailed the waters and this little archipelago became known as Carteret Group for want of any other name, but the natives living there knew it as 'Kilinailau'. At Seven that morning some of these inhabitants were seen approaching the ship; they came in their canoes quite close enough in fact to see that it was a well built craft with a large outrigger. The crew consisted of nine true Melanesians, all of them black, woolly-headed, sturdy men, quite naked as for as they could see and armed with bows and arrows. For a moment it appeared as if they were about to attack, but unaccountably thought better of it, laying down their arms in the boat again. Even then, in spite of welcoming signs from the crew of the *Swallow*, they declined to come any closer and soon after continued on their way. Later several other canoes approached with their sails set but gave the ship a wide berth.

On Tuesday August 25th James Fogarty, one of the marines died, another victim of the Egmont Isle native's arrows. At 11.30 that morning his body was committed to the deep. It was a day of light winds with the *Swallow* making slow progress westward and being so much at the mercy of the current was found to be some twenty miles north of her estimated position and a short distance from a long low island. It was 10 o'clock in the evening watch and too dark to make out any details, but daylight next morning revealed an island nine miles in length having a covering of bright green vegetation which Carteret, thinking it to be a new discovery, named after Sir Charles Hardy. In fact it had been seen by Le Maire and Schouten a century and a half before and named by them "Greene Eylanden".

The following day, Wednesday 26th, the day when Carteret felt sufficiently recovered to come out on deck and resume full command, the breeze was light and fluky and he had difficulty getting the *Swallow* clear of Green Island. It was 7 o'clock next morning before he was able to coax her back on a course heading towards New Britain. But now with the breeze so light the north-going current held sway and her progress was sideways rather than forward and even with every stitch of canvas set, progress was rarely seen to be more than one knot when the log was streamed. The morning of the 27th found the *Swallow* within sight of islands to the north and at the same time what appeared to be more islands to the west. These were the waters where earlier explorer's tracks crossed: Drake, Magellan, Tasman, Le Maire and Dampier all passed this way, giving their particular names to islands and headlands later to be rediscovered and bestowed with new names, many of which are now disregarded in favour of indigenous ones.

The current which so relentlessly bore the *Swallow* northwards now changed, rebounding off the mainland and setting her to the south-west. At noon a headland was seen which Carteret concluded was the one Dampier sighted on St George's Day in 1700 and so named. Beyond this headland lay St George's Bay where Carteret pinned his hopes on finding a sheltered anchorage. As the *Swallow* closed the land, the hummocks which earlier had been mistaken for islands turned out, on approach, to be the jungle covered hills and mountains of the mainland of New Britain. Progress continued to be slow, the breeze so frustratingly light and variable fell to a calm leaving the *Swallow*, her sails idle and drooping, drifting without movement save when some trick of the current swung her slowly through all the points of the compass. In the early hours of the morning, Friday August 28th, when at last the land breeze came away, her speed picked up a little, two or three knots by the log and the morning watch found her abreast of Cape St George where the sea on the weather side broke continually. Beyond this the shore was seen to trend to the north-west, revealing a sheltered coast-line with an island at the entrance to a deep bay offering the real possibility of a safe haven.

It had been a long drawn out reach in continually light winds with Cape St George always in sight for the past twenty-four hours and now, having seen much promise close at hand, Carteret wore ship immediately and stood in towards the island with the deep-sea lead going all the time but no bottom, not even at 130 fathoms within two miles of the shore. At 8.30 Gower was sent with the cutter to examine the bay and at 10 o'clock he made a sign that he had struck soundings but with coral bottom and poor holding ground. At six bells, much to the relief of all hands, another signal was seen that a good mooring was to be had in between the shore and the island. This island, which Carteret named after Captain Wallis, was described as barren with sandy beaches and a few coconut trees. It formed the northern shore of the entrance to the bay which was quite narrow, the width between the island and the mainland being less than a mile. The breeze at this time was unfavourable, but with the *Swallow* close hauled on the port tack she might make it to the anchorage.

Giving the order to hoist out the long boat, he sent her ahead to lead the way, then following after on a taut bowline he conned the *Swallow* into the bay as far as was possible under the prevailing conditions and just before noon, he backed the mainyards and brought her to with the best bower in 37 fathoms and the stream anchor aft, a quarter of a mile from the shore of the mainland. When this was done the topgallant yards were sent down and the ship secured in all respects for the night.

Taking stock of his surroundings, Carteret noted that at

present there was no sign of inhabitants. The mainland, although jungle, should yield vegetables, but anyway there would be coconuts and the bay should yield plenty of fish. Furthermore turtles had been seen on the beaches of Wallis Island as the *Swallow* approached the anchorage and these, when caught would make good eating. In the meantime, the cutter was sent off to search out a suitable berth to careen the ship.

When she returned at 5 o'clock that afternoon, Gower was able to report that a cove had been found where the *Swallow* could lie comfortably with trees at hand to take her moorings. The cove was conveniently situated at the mouth of a small river with plenty of wood and shingle for ballast if required. Altogether it appeared ideally suited but it was now 5 p.m. too late to shift ship to new moorings, but still time enough for the long boat to go to Wallis Island for coconuts. This was done and soon the boats crew were wielding their axes, bringing the trees crashing down, all fourteen of them eventually, requiring several journeys to ferry the nuts and the green cabbage-like tops back to the ship.

By midnight the weather turned wet with heavy tropical rainfall and continued throughout the middle watch, but by 5 o'clock it had cleared. When unmooring commenced, first recovering the sheet anchor, the cable on the bower was hove short. At seven, the topgallant yards were sent up and at eight, the capstan was manned in preparation to finally get under weigh.

With the cable hove short on the bower, all hands could expect to be moving shortly to the new mooring and it would have been so had the anchor not become foul. As it was, breakfast had been delayed and would have to wait until the anchor was cleared. Perhaps fitter men might have broken it out, but scurvy was taking its toll with some of the seamen lacking in vigour. Obviously more purchase was required and the cat tackle, according to Kerton's account, "was clap't on to the cable" and taken to the capstan and hove but to no effect. To this was added the top tackle with no improvement and at this stage, cutting the cable was considered but firmly rejected owing to cable and anchor being irreplaceable. As a last resort, a viol[21] was secured to the anchor cable, and with the sheet cable used as a runner it was taken to the capstan. With these three purchases the capstan was manned again expecting that this would do the trick, yet sweat and strain at the bars as they might, the cable would not budge an inch.

It was now decided to leave things as they were and try again later. At any rate at last the crew could go for their breakfast, not a particularly appetising one which consisted of no more than portable broth and boiled coconut cabbage. In the end their exertions were spared and at noon the purchases were removed and the cable veered out with the hope that it would clear itself at the turn of the tide, which it did, coming home next morning with no bother at all when the capstan was manned. However, between then and now the boats were sent off, the cutter to catch fish and the long boat for coconuts and cabbage. There were plenty of fish around, those on the cutter could see them, and although the seine was set in a ring round the shoals, when it was pursed, it fouled the uneven coral bed and the fish escaped. This happened more than once, returning to the ship only four small fish. However they brought news that there were turtles on the sandy beaches of Wallis Island, so a few men were put ashore that evening to catch them. They stayed there all night, but when they were picked up next morning they had to report that they had not seen any.

Dawn on Sunday August 30th came in quietly with not a breath of wind. If time was not to be wasted, the *Swallow* must

---

[21] A 'viol' is a rope of smaller circumference than the anchor cable which is made fast to the anchor cable and then taken to the capstan. Often called a 'messenger'. The reason for this is that the anchor cable is too large in circumference to be rove round the capstan.

be towed to her new berth. Both cutter and long boat were launched and sent ahead with their tow-ropes made fast. At 5.30 the capstan was manned and to their surprise, the anchor came home. It was found to have one of its flukes or blades, as Kerton calls them, badly damaged. Meanwhile towing commenced, but progress was slow and even if the boats oars were double-banked, they did not achieve much headway. Then someone remembered the sweeps, those great unwieldy oars stowed on the poop. The rowing ports, nine inches square, were there in the bulwarks, ten on each side and although some of the sweeps had been lost overboard earlier in the voyage, the remainder were shipped and rowing commenced. They were ponderous things those sweeps, twenty, maybe twenty-five feet in length, each one needing three or four men to handle them, but even with their added power of propulsion, progress was desperately slow, four miles at the most in three hours of labour and by 9 o'clock, they still had not reached the cove and it must have raised a cheer from those at the oars when a light breeze from the north-west filled the tops'ls and helped them on their way. At last at 9.30 they came to anchor at the entrance to the cove. The *Swallow* was then warped in and moored with anchors fore and aft, and when this was done two 4 1/2 inch hawsers were carried ashore and made fast to trees, one on either side, in order to steady her in the berth.

Here at last was a place where the *Swallow* could lie safely while being careened and repaired, where her immediate needs were to be found, wood, water, fruit, green vegetables and fish in plenty.

Another important point was there appeared to be no hostile natives to attack them. The crew would be busy but there would be time to relax. All hands, particularly those sick with the scurvy would gather strength for the next part of the voyage. The *Swallow* and her crew had now sailed more than half way round the world. If all went well they would soon reach the Dutch East Indies, the nearest civilisation, Batavia or Surabaya, where the ship would be repaired and restocked and ready to set off round the Cape of Good Hope for home. Carteret gave this cove the name of English Harbour.

Chapter IX

Once the *Swallow* was safely moored in English Harbour, Carteret set the crew to work on the various tasks urgently required to be completed in order to continue the voyage before the changes of the 'south-east monsoon'. There were now between twenty and thirty men on the sick-list suffering from scurvy, leaving only two thirds of the ship's company, few of whom were in really good health and able to do the work.

The harbour was as perfect as could be expected for careening the ship, a natural dock 200 feet in length with tress available along the bank to set up the careening tackle. Beyond the shore line were hills and mountains up to 2,000ft or more, jungle covered, with a variety of trees amongst which Carteret expected to find some sort of fruit. Up until now no inhabitants had been perceived, but there were marks on coconuts trees to be seen, and he was taking no chances by ensuring that the shore parties always had a marine, armed guard or sentinel to accompany them. As a further precaution, he sent a working party ashore to clear away the undergrowth around the little harbour, to give an open view from the ship and reduce the chance of a surprise attack.

On Tuesday work started in earnest. This was the first day of September, and with the season so far advanced, there was not a moment to be lost. The cutter was sent off to catch fish with the seine net, and then to bring back coconuts of which there were plenty, and the crash of coconut trees coming down became a frequent sound along the shore for the next few days. They also brought back with them the green shoots from the top of the tree. Some of the crew were sent ashore to cut wood for the galley stove, others to fill casks from the stream at the top end of the little harbour; those not engaged in these duties, were set to work clearing the holds in preparation to careening by rousing out the empty casks and starting the salt water butts used for ballast, all to be refilled with fresh water in due course. Anything else in the way of ship's stores which could safely be removed was sent ashore, and having done all this, the topgallant masts were struck, purchases rigged from the topmastheads to trees on the larboard side, and when ready, all hands tailed on the purchases and the *Swallow* was hove down in order to come at the leak on the starboard bow.

At the same time the crew were set to cleaning as much of the weeds and marine growth off the hull as possible and when the ship's side was sufficiently exposed on the starboard side, the carpenter, the redoubtable John Renshaw, a man who appeared to have more energy than most in spite of his 54 years, set to work on repairs to the leak. When the starboard side had been dealt with, the ship was turned end for end and hove down to get at the larboard side. This was the daily routine followed by the crew for the next few days. When the repairs and cleaning were completed on the starboard side the ship was turned end to end an again hove down to get at the marine growth on the starboard side.

Carteret only rarely appeared to set foot on shore. However with regard to the crew, in addition to wood and waterers, he sent all those ashore who were on the sick list and able to walk in order to gain benefit from the open air and sunshine. He set great store in this and also in the value of the coconuts for combating scurvy, also the green cabbage tops, although much of the goodness was lost in the boiling. But before all hands went ashore, he saw that they were fed at breakfast with portable soup and coconuts. It had been expected that this diet would be enhanced by the addition of fish of which there were plenty in the bay, but neither cutters nor the long boat appeared to be able to catch any, however hard they tried. But they later did, on one occasion, return with oysters. Lieutenant Gower when no engaged with the cutter's crew chopping down coconut trees or fishing, employed himself in surveying the coastline and taking observations to be recorded later on a chart.

On board the *Swallow*, as the task of cleaning her hull progressed, it was found that beneath the marine growth accumulated since Chatham, not only was the wooden sheathing decayed, but the ship's bottom itself much eaten by worms. With thirty or forty men employed scraping off the strakes and coating them with a mixture of pitch and tar, the job was done in three days, Kerton tells us, in spite of delays by rain showers. What life was like for those whose duties and infirmities kept them aboard, a ship heeled to an angle of thirty or forty degrees, he does not say, but there were no complaints recorded, not even from the cooks who would have had to take their pots and pans ashore to boil the crew's salt beef by a wood fire on the beach.

On Thursday morning in the small hours, Matthew Wright died of tetanus and the lockjaw which followed from wounds received during Simpson's disastrous expedition at Egmont Island. Simpson himself was ill with his wounds, another case of tetanus which was soon to carry him away. Seaman Wright had a Christian funeral and was buried ashore at 11 o'clock that morning.

The careening was completed this day and the *Swallow* once again brought to an even keel. Now began the task of loading and re-stowing casks of water, barrels of salt beef and pork, all hoisted aboard with a block and whip at the yardarm. After this was done, there was the wood for the galley, spars, hawsers and all the gear in the careening to be brought aboard. So much of the stores which came aboard in Chatham had been consumed that the *Swallow's* fore and aft trim was so altered to make her poor sailing qualities even worse. However, the means of putting this right was at hand. The stream which flowed into the little harbour deposited some fine shingle on a bank within easy reach. What better could there be than this, if stowed in the right part of the hold to restore, or perhaps improve her sailing qualities? Altogether twelve tons were brought on board for this purpose. However, even with this additional weight aft the ship was still too much by the head, so some of the crew were given the job of shifting the iron ballast in the coal hole situated right in the eyes of the ship, to the after end of the hold. Whether all this would improve matters, only time would tell.

At least this period in English Harbour brought a small measure of improvement in the health of the crew: to be in the open air away from the foetid atmosphere of the tween deck was of great benefit, and Carteret continued to encourage all those able to do so to go ashore in the cool of the evening to bathe or walk in the wood. Kerton, in company with others, ventured three miles up a dry watercourse searching for fruit as an alternative for the everlasting coconut and cabbage. There was always the hope that scurvy grass or something similar might be found, but there was none.

However, on one of his expeditions, Kerton came across a tall tree resembling the West Indian 'Jamaica Plum' which, if any quantity could have been found, would have proved useful as an anti-scorbutic, but there was no time to search for more. Other fruits trees were seen, but their names were not known, apart from the nutmeg which yielded a quantity of nuts to be carried back aboard. As far as vegetables were concerned, the only ones found were the wild yam and potato, neither of which were deemed edible. Of wild life there were pigeons, doves, rooks and parrots, so Carteret tells us, and a mysterious large bird which made a noise like the barking of a dog! Very few animals were seen; only two creatures like small dogs or jackals, but some of the crew heard a sound like that of a lion, and others who visited the same place were willing to confirm that it might well have been so.

By now the various tasks on board the *Swallow* were nearing completion, giving a period of comparative leisure. Carteret found time to venture ashore where he sowed seeds of many different sorts, just as Anson did before him on Juan Fernandez Island. He does not mention this in his Journal, but Kerton recorded it in his Log. He also makes note of the various trees available, cane being one of them, not much use to the carpenters but there were others yielding timber of a quality from which they could fashion stuns'l booms, something which the *Swallow* was always in need of, and also spare booms for the steering sail. Strange to relate, no native inhabitants were seen. The evidence was there of their visits not only by nature of the marked coconut trees, but some huts were found, poorly fashioned and not inhabited at present, but discarded seashells and traces of recent fires indicated that their owners might return at any time to wreak vengeance for such wanton destruction of their property. Carteret was very conscious of this. Thus, when Gower returned from a surveying expedition in the cutter with the report that he had found an excellent anchorage three leagues up the coast, he decided to leave English Harbour as soon as possible.

Further inquiry confirmed Carteret's decision. The bay, which became known as Carteret Harbour, appeared ideal for completing the repairs; plenty of wood available, also fresh water nearby, and most important, a good berth close to the beach where the *Swallow's* guns could command the foreshore in the event of any attack by the natives. From then on everything was put in hand to prepare the ship to get under weigh first thing next morning, each item taken ashore to lighten the ship had to be brought back on board; water casks, full or empty, barrels and boxes of ship's stores together with wood for the galley, spars, hawsers and all the gear used in careening.

While all this was going on there was one particular task to be done, namely to complete the formality of taking possession of all the surrounding land, islands, ports and harbours in the name of His Britannic Majesty, King George III of Great

Britain, all of which was engraved on a plaque including Carteret's name and that of the *Swallow*. When completed and suitably enhanced by being painted red, white and blue, it was nailed to the highest tree in a prominent position for all to see.

Next morning, Monday, September 7th, at 6.30, with the assistance of the cutter, the stream anchor was weighed, and while the longboat fetched the last tun of water remaining on shore, the capstan was manned and the cable on the bower anchor hove short. This done, at 7 o'clock the careening hawsers were cast off and the *Swallow*, with a fair wind ran clear out of the harbour into the channel where the braces were manned, the helm put down and the ship steadied WNW towards a headland four miles distant. The breeze was NNE and with the ship close hauled on the starboard tack, she was soon abreast of the headland, giving a wide berth to the shoal water and dangerous rock awash two cables to seaward. Once clear of this, with the longboat in the lead taking soundings as she went, the course was directed into the bay which Gower had recently surveyed. Progress was slow in the prevailing light breeze and she did not reach the top end of the bay until the end of the morning watch, where the cutter waited to signal the best mooring. Finally, at noon, the *Swallow* came to anchor in 33 fathoms with good mud bottom.

The bay and the mooring was just as Gower had described it to Carteret, better in fact being sheltered as it was from the north and the east by the jungle-covered hills of the main land, and from the west and the south by two islands. The smaller one to the south was named after the purser, Edward Leigh, while the larger to the north became Coconut Isle, one and a half miles long with hills 800 feet high giving shelter from west to south. Its perimeter was surrounded by an amazing number of coconut trees, hence the name Carteret gave it. When the anchor was let go, the cable was veered away and the ship steadied with the kedge anchor out aft, and was finally brought up lying within s quarter of a cable's length from the coconut trees. On the other side of the bay, half a mile to the north, was an inlet or cove where there was a suitable run of water available. This was aptly named Watering Bay.

However, water not being a priority at this time, both the cutter and the longboat, with a party of 30 men between them, armed against any natives, were sent off at 2 o'clock that afternoon to gather coconuts and green shoots, and soon they were causing mayhem with the trees as a large number was felled to obtain them, and when the two boats returned, they brought with them 750 nuts. Later, each man was issued four. That night the *Swallow* lay peacefully at her moorings. The trade wind blew moderately while tropical lightning flickered in the west over Coconut Isle. Carteret, anxious as ever to proceed with the voyage so long delayed, allowed only one more day to complete wood and watering.

First thing next morning, the cutter and longboat went for more coconuts returning at 10 o'clock with a further 350, each crew member being issued with three. In the afternoon, the cutter was sent to take soundings in the channel between Coconut Isle and the opposite shore. She was soon back again with the news that there was a good depth of water and no dangers bordering either shore, and offering a clear passage to seaward. It was Carteret's intention to go that way and take the *Swallow* deep into St George's Bay where he considered he might find a passage through to the north. In this respect, he was guided by the strong current which flowed into the bay, deeming that there must be an outlet for it somewhere to the north.

Dampier came this way in 1699 on a voyage of discovery in *H.M.S. Roebuck*. After surveying part of the west coast of Australia, he came via Timor, to New Guinea. Then, skirting the northern coast he reached the island which he named Nova Britannica. Passing South of this, he entered a stretch of water, and considering it to be a bay, he named it after St George. He then continued his way following a course east about, returning to Timor. If indeed there was a channel through at the top of St George's Bay, it would save fourteen days on passage to

Batavia, and since time was now of paramount importance, Carteret decided to take a chance of finding it. He was anxious to be gone and allowed only one more night at the anchorage. Although the sojourn in Gower Harbour and Carteret Bay had been of benefit to both the ship and crew, as far as the latter was concerned, scurvy still held sway; affecting 26 men at this time. There were also six men ill from arrow wounds including Simpson, and a further two men down with fever. Carteret himself was still in a bad way, but with neither of the midshipmen nor master's mates able to take Simpson's place, he was forced to go watch and watch with Gower. It was only great determination that kept him to this duty, for not only did he do his four hours on deck, but he had to be available in his watch below for any particular call requiring his presence.

Next morning, Thursday, September 9th, all hands were called at 4 a.m., at least all those fit enough to turn out, to man the capstan and weigh the anchor. The wind being ENE, it was doubtful whether the *Swallow* could weather Coconut Isle, so the kedge was slung under the cutter with a girtline and several turns of cable coiled down on the after thwarts ready to be paid out, as she was rowed towards the mainland where the kedge was dropped close to the shore. She was now in far better shape than when she arrived on the coast: leak reduced; rigging taut; water casks filled, and although the decks were somewhat cluttered with wood for the galley together with hundreds of coconuts not yet struck down below for want of space, she was as ready to go as ever she would be. At 6 o'clock, the capstan was manned, and with all hands in good spirits at the prospect of getting to sea again, they hove away with a will, and when the bower anchor was aweigh, the sails were sheeted home, even those of the crew on the sick list lending a hand with what strength they could muster. Then the kedge was taken to the capstan, and when the *Swallow* was hove sufficiently to windward, the sails were filled and she cleared Coconut Isle by a safe margin.

Chapter X

Wishing to get a good offing, Carteret set the course to the west. The wind was light and variable to start with, and not until noon was the *Swallow* able to be brought to bear up northerly towards where the hoped for Strait would be found. Early in the afternoon, she was suddenly taken all aback, however, soon after this the breeze came away fresh from the east and thereafter, the speed picked up until the second dog watch when once again the breeze deserted them. A canoe was sighted this morning, the first to be seen on this coast, a small one with two natives in it, but no contact was established with them.

Once clear of Carteret Point the coast to the east could be seen to trend northward while on the other side of the bay, now plainly visible, showed up in the form of three distinctive hummocks on either side, all three being aptly named The Mother and Daughters. Both sides of the bay were covered in jungle as far as the eye could see, but there was a remarkable difference in as much as the western coast appeared to have a population, and a degree of cultivation quite lacking on the eastern side where the only natives seen were those in the canoe earlier on.

By now it was becoming clear to Carteret that his hunch of a passage at the top of St George's Bay was a good one, since what appeared to be a continuous coastline ahead turned out to be an island in the middle of a strait about twenty-five miles across at its widest part. This was a wonderful source of satisfaction, an important discovery and one which saved him and the *Swallow* a weary beat of several 100 miles by going round the south coast of New Britain. He wrote in his Journal.

"I found it a large Channell or Straits clear of all dangers as far as I saw, so instead of this being only an Island, I found it to be two large Islands."

He refers to New Britain on the western side and gives the other island to the east the name of New Ireland or Hibernia as he sometimes called it.

Early that evening the weather came in foul and thick, and by now it was too late to attempt to explore any further: sail was shortened and the ship hove to for the night, first on the starboard tack until midnight when., with all hands on deck, they wore her round onto the port tack. Eventually the weather cleared and it became a fine tropical night. And now there was evidence of more people in these northern parts of New Ireland as fires could be seen and the sound of drums borne on the breeze continued to be heard throughout the night as if the natives never slept.

At 4 a.m. before the first glimmer of dawn, the reefs were shaken out and the *Swallow's* course set towards the north. It was Friday, September 11th. The breeze was light and progress slow, two knots no more, and plenty of time to study the island and the mainland beyond. At 8 a.m. it became clear that passages through the strait existed on both sides of the island, but the one to the east appeared to be clear of any dangers, while in the western reaches a number of islets could be seen. Thus, in view of the *Swallow's* unhandiness in confined waters, Carteret decided to take the eastern passage. He named the island after the Duke of York. On the port hand, between Duke of York Island and a point of land known as Cape Gazelle, lay a sheltered bay with a clear view of two distinctive hills on the far side, called Mother and Daughter, volcanoes at one time but now extinct. In fact, much of the coastline round the bay was volcanic, if mainly dormant, but smoke from an active one could be seen beyond the Mother and Daughter. The bay offered good anchorage, and a sheltered cove at the top end became known as Simpson Harbour where the busy port of Rabaul was later established.

Nine o'clock found the *Swallow* well within the eastern passage referred to as the Narrows, a stretch of water twenty miles wide. By noon she was halfway through, and it became clear to Carteret that the northern extremity of New Britain had been reached, but the coast of New Ireland extended even further, trending in a north-westerly direction onwards into the far distance.

A study of Duke of York Island revealed it to be long and low, about twenty miles from north to south described by Carteret as well-inhabited, full of coconut plantations and houses. Kerton had more to say maintaining that it was very pleasant with small houses near the beach, each with a kind of palisade. There appeared to be no dangerous rocks or reefs and many fine canoes were drawn up on the beach. There were people there, black inhabitants gathered on the foreshore armed with spears and later some canoes were launched and these followed the *Swallow* for a while but could not keep up with her and soon returned to their village.

It was 6 o'clock that evening when the *Swallow* cleared north end of Duke of York Island revealing a view to the west where another smaller island was seen and given the name of Isle of Man. Beyond the island was a headland which marked the northern extremity of New Britain with open water as far as the eye could see. The Dutch East Indies, Carteret's intended destination, lay 3,000 miles away, but the wind was fair and sail after sail was piled on in order to make the best speed possible. The course set was North-West by West and this was continued throughout the night while maintaining a safe distance off the New Ireland Coast. As the evening wore on the breeze freshened and by the end of the watch it was blowing a gale with the *Swallow* reefed right down. The night was unusually black with flashes of lightning followed by great claps of thunder and this continued until the early hours when the weather moderated and the sails were set once again.

Around six bells in the morning watch a fleet of canoes was seen approaching. The breeze was light at the time and with the *Swallow* barely making headway she was soon overtaken and surrounded by a dozen or more, some of which paddled up within hailing distance. These craft came from the coast of New Ireland, quite the largest seen so far, and Carteret noted that one canoe in particular was amazingly long being about the same length as the *Swallow*, some 80 or 90 feet in fact, with a crew of 33 men on board. She was a narrow craft, obviously hewn out of the trunk of one tree, having an outrigger to steady her but no sails. Their ropes appeared to be well made and the hull was decorated with carved ornaments. He also noted that the natives were similar to those on Egmont Island, quite naked except for ornaments on their arms and legs. They had beads and woolly hair which they bleached with a white powder and also made use of paints to decorate their faces. Altogether they appeared quite wary, not coming too close to the ship as if they had knowledge of fire arms. Nonetheless, the guns were cleared and made ready with the crew at quarters in case an attack should come. After a while they approached close enough to exchange a few trifling things which they did by means of long sticks. They showed interest in all kinds of iron. With regard to weapons, they had spears and if indeed they possessed bows and arrows, they kept them well concealed. It was hoped that they might go and get some coconuts to barter with but with no result, and after a while the wind freshened, and seeing that there was nothing further to be gained, Carteret gave the order to bear away.

The canoes ceased to follow and were soon left far astern, not that the *Swallow* was making any great progress, and in spite of all the hours spent cleaning the hull at English Cove, she could not be coaxed to greater speed, only 84 miles on the 12th, even with a good current in her favour. The noon position by a reliable meridian altitude of the sun put the *Swallow* ten miles off shore, a distance which Carteret maintained to be well clear of any rock or reef which might be encountered as she coasted along. Here was the opportunity to do a running survey of the shore with the *Swallow* pottering along at two or three knots, but everything was against this. "I am conscious," he wrote in his Journal when referring his shortcomings, "I found the duty too much for me, who was very sickly and ailing....so weak that I could scarcely keep the deck." Surely a good time to delegate responsibility: among the warrant officers or master's mates there should be someone qualified, or at least capable of taking a watch, and under the circumstances it is to be wondered at his perseverance in combining his duties as Captain with those of a watchkeeper. Watch and watch entails ten hours one day followed by fourteen hours on the next, a very wearing routine under normal conditions, and present conditions were far from normal.

The weather turned stormy in the afternoon with a great swell coming up from the south, and at half past two the crew wore ship to the south in order to clear a large island to leewards which Carteret gave the name Prince of Wales Island. By noon the following day the *Swallow* was abreast of the western end of the mainland where just beyond the point lay another island. The channel between this and the mainland was named Byron Strait while the island beyond became New Hanover. The weather at this time continued unsettled with frequent squalls which sometimes reached gale force with the *Swallow* down to reefed tops'ls and all three topgallant yards and masts struck down. In one of the squalls the mains'l was badly split and had to be sent down for repairs. The marines, when not assisting with handling sails, employed themselves cleaning their small arms. Also, at the quieter moments, the seamen were engaged in drawing and knotting yarns.

Next day, Monday, September 15th at four bells in the morning watch, land was sighted bearing WNW and the *Swallow* was immediately hauled up for it. The weather by now had moderated with the topgallant masts and yards once again hoisted and the ship proceeding under all sail. At first what appeared at a distance to be a large rock, on approach broadened out to be an island at the centre of an archipelago, the extent of which was discovered later that evening. Gower was on watch at the time, and as luck would have it, the night was clear and moonlit, and he realised that the *Swallow* was heading into a cluster of small islets and rocks and in danger of running aground on an unseen reef. He immediately altered course on his own account, not wishing to call his Captain out as he would be coming on watch in another hour, something which pleased Carteret. An hour after he did come on watch he was able to see that the ship was clear of the southernmost islet and brought the *Swallow* back on her westerly course. He named this archipelago Admiralty Islands.

Soon after daylight the first sign that the Admiralty Islands were inhabited was the appearance of canoes with unusual slanting, rectangular sails, the larger ones having two masts. At first there were only a few canoes whose occupants were curious to see this strange vessel. It is doubtful if they had ever encountered one before, although such a ship might exist in their folklore since Le Maire and Schouteri had visited these waters in 1616 and Saavedra, the Spanish navigator, a century earlier. Gower had the morning watch, but he had Carteret called out from his watch below and preparations were made to receive them. There was always the hope they might be friendly, but in case they were not, the marines and some of the seamen were ready with loaded muskets while others stood by to use the swivels or main armament if required. As the canoes approached, the nearest one with five natives on board was seen to be making signs which those on the *Swallow* took to be amicable and did their best to imitate in the hope that they would come on board; they also held out some articles for gifts or barter, but the result of all this was an unexpected volley of spears as soon as they came within range. They were primitive weapons, these spears, with sharp flint tips which fortunately wounded nobody, but were thrown with such force as to stick firmly in the *Swallow's* timbers.

This would not do. Other canoes were approaching and with the *Swallow* barely having steerage way, she would soon be overtaken. In order to deter another attack Carteret ordered a musket volley to be fired over their heads, but with no effect, so a second volley was ordered. This was more effective in as much as some of the crew, disregarding orders to fire high, aimed at their bodies hitting two of them, at which they paddled off as fast as they were able in order to join the fleet of canoes gathering from many different islands in the archipelago. It now looked as if another attack was imminent.

The second one when it came brought altogether a much larger number of canoes. It was going to be a close run thing whether or not the *Swallow*'s crew could hold them off. If they reached the ship's side, would the crew be able to repel boarders with one third of the ship's complement on the sick list? A much more forthright deterrent was urgently required. Another musket volley and a swivel gun fired over their heads might serve, so this was done immediately with no effect whatsoever. And now the crew were firing into the boats, wounding, even killing their assailants. But still they came on, the first of them near enough to throw their spears before leaping into the water, and swimming back to a cluster of large canoes which seemed all set to launch another attack, despite the deadly treatment from the *Swallow*'s muskets.

Now that there was no hope of peaceful commerce, the safety of the ship was the priority, needing the main armament. Ordering the six pounders to be run out, Carteret directed the gunner to fire a broadside over their heads, and in the end this had the desired effect. The loud report and 'swoosh' of the balls passing over them marked the end of their resolution, and immediately they hoisted their sails and paddled away to the shore as fast as they could.

One more opportunity of a friendly rapport with the islanders offered itself later that morning when a canoe, returning from a fishing expedition, came within hailing distance. It was, as it turned out, a poor somewhat primitive craft with a sail of matting and an outrigger, manned by six black woolly-headed natives. The *Swallow*, with little more than steerageway, came slowly up to the canoe with the crew making the usual signs of friendship, but as Kerton tells us, with no favourable outcome. Not even the offer of gifts tempted them. They sat in silence resting their paddles as they watched the ship until the moment when she was close enough, when they stood up and hove their spears at her hull where they stuck quivering in the timbers of her quarter. Meanwhile the cutter was launched as a means of further friendly approach. However this was no better. When she came close enough the crew were met with a hail of spears hurled with deadly intent.

The reply from the cutter was predictable. A ragged musket volley by the seamen ended any hope of parley, and when they came up to the canoe, two of the natives were seen to be dead and two others wounded. But, injured or not, the remaining four leaped overboard and swam for the shore leaving their canoe to be captured by the cutter and hoisted on board the *Swallow*.

This was a truly sad state of affairs: another archipelago and a complete failure to establish friendly relations. Almost within their grasp were all they required; fruit, fish and probably good red meat available to bring the crew back to health again, a later study of the canoe's contents pointed to this. Yet in spite of the failure to make friends with the islanders, Carteret gave a good account of the archipelago allowing that the islands, if a successful approach were to be made and friendly relations established, were undoubtedly favourable for trading with other vessels in the future. The *Swallow* was close enough to see plenty of coconut trees, and also land which appeared to be cultivated. He described the inhabitants as woolly-headed, black or copper coloured negroes and nearly the same as those of Nova Hibernia and Egmont Island. He observed that they went about quite naked apart from adorning themselves with shells and toys, and that they chewed betelnut. 'They seem to be,' he wrote, 'a wild, fierce savage people.' He regretted very much that on account of the nature of the inhabitants he was unable to examine the archipelago more thoroughly. He estimated that there were between 20 and 30 islands, the largest 50 to 60 miles in length. He gave the position to be 2° 18' south 146° 44' east.[22]

With such an unfriendly reception there was no point in persevering further, so the *Swallow* was once again put on her westerly course. But progress was poor, taking four days to cover the next hundred miles, the season at this time being near the Equinox and unsettled weather conditions with squalls, calms and shifts of wind which frequently caught the ship aback. At any rate there was plenty of leisure to study the captured canoe. It was the smallest they had seen so far, 49 feet, hewn out of a single log. Carteret's opinion of it was a poor one, being coarse and ill made with one outrigger to steady it. The sails were made of matting, and over the outrigger was a shelter fashioned from curved witheys covered with matting. Kerton made a note of the contents in his log: two earthenware vessels which he called 'cudgery pots', one of which had been on a small fire cooking the natives' breakfast. There were yams and a small fruit like a guava which when roasted was very good and tasted like a sweet potato. There were also ten large fishes and a turtle of about 40 lbs. Neither Carteret nor Kerton considered the canoe worth keeping and when the inspection was completed, it was sawn up for firewood to be burnt in the galley fire.

The early hours of the following morning, Friday September 17th, were particularly wearisome. Soon after midnight the call

---

[22] At this point Carteret is only 16 minutes out, the correct longitude being 147° 00' E.

came for "all hands on deck" when a violent thunderstorm threatened to blow all the sails to shreds. All those who were well enough to do so tumbled out of their hammocks and were soon aloft battling with the canvas. First the mizen-topsail was furled, then the fore and main topsail were reefed. Thereafter it was the turn of both courses to be clewed up and stowed. By 1.30 the wind had eased sufficiently for the reefs to be shaken out and the sails set again after which peace reigned for a while. But not for long however. At 2 o'clock the *Swallow* was taken aback, requiring more attention to the sails. At 3 o'clock calm set in and this continued until 6 o'clock, when the breeze came away and soon she was under all sail again. At breakfast she was suddenly taken aback for a second time followed by all the hauling and belaying of sheets and braces entailed to get her on course again.

The sky remained overcast and no noon observation was taken. At 9 o'clock in the evening Alexander Simpson, the Master, passed away. He never recovered from the wounds received at Egmont Island, although one day he felt well enough to go fishing in the cutter. Soon after this the fatal 'lock-jaw' set in. He was the last one to die as a result of that abortive expedition. Soon after this sad event the ship was struck by a tornado with all hands taking in sail and snugging her down in the expectation of another stormy night, sending down topgallant and royal yards and finally striking the spritsail topsail itself. It was a dark, windy and thundery night and it continued unsettled until the end of the middle watch. The ship remained under reduced sail until breakfast time when the yards were sent up again, and all sails set once more. At noon that day the body of Simpson was committed to the deep. Three volleys of small arms were fired in his honour.

Taking in sail each night reduced the day's run, but at least the current was in the *Swallow*'s favour, increasing her westward progress by about 24 miles from noon to noon. On Sunday evening a long, low island was sighted almost right ahead, but not until it was quite close, and soon after this the lookout at the masthead reported another island to the starboard, an estimated distance of twenty to twenty-five miles. The northern island whose Melanesian name is Aua, was given the name of an acquaintance of Carteret's, a Mr Duroure, and the long low island to the south, Wuvulu in the native tongue, became Matty's Island, named after Mr Matthew Matty, the Secretary of the Royal Society and a personal friend of Carteret's. However, it turned out that neither island was a new discovery, having been sighted by Orthes de Retes as long ago as 1545 and named by him Islas de Hombres Blanco. It was too late in the day to investigate either of these islands, and anyway, with the recent reception by the islanders still fresh in their memory, it seemed advisable not to do so. All that night, as the *Swallow* sailed along the coast of Matty's Island, the natives followed the shore, carrying brightly burning torches, whether welcome or warning was a matter of conjecture, and as the wind was fair Carteret decided not to investigate further.

With the breeze and current in her favour, the *Swallow* covered the next 400 miles in four days. On Tuesday, September 22nd, Thomas Allen, one of the seamen, died. He had been suffering from scurvy for some time, and sensing that he might not recover, he made a will leaving all his effects to his messmate, seaman Michael Walker. Apart from an entry in his log to this effect, Kerton found little of interest to record. The routine of snugging down the ship for the night continued, and one day he noted that a cask of salt beef, no: 923 was opened and found to be woefully short of a number of pieces, the result of skulduggery back in Deptford. On Thursday he recorded that logs were frequently sighted drifting by and more seabirds than usual flying around the ship, a sure sign of land somewhere below the horizon.

Sure enough early next morning two islands were sighted from the masthead to the south, but too far off to warrant investigation. Carteret named them the Stephens Islands after the Admiralty Secretary, Stephens. The native names were Ajawi in 0° 11'S 135° 00'E and Beponde in 0° 25'S 135 °16'E.

There were plenty of fish around the ship at this time, and a turtle was seen, also sharks, two of which were caught and later served out to all hands for their dinner. The following day more islands were sighted. It was Saturday, September 26th, a day to remember, the first that a worthwhile encounter with native Pacific islanders was achieved.

It was 5 o'clock in the morning watch when a further three islands were seen to the north. It had been a frustrating day with a light variable breeze, and soon after breakfast the *Swallow* was caught all aback and had to be wore round on the other tack. Just before noon, land was sighted and the course was immediately altered towards it. It turned out to be another island covered with trees which appeared "rising out of the sea like ships," as Kerton wrote. Beyond it two other islands were seen, much smaller than the first, and all three were surrounded by a reef. The direction of the wind together with the set and drift of the current, was causing the *Swallow* to make so much leeway that there seemed little likelihood of bringing her close enough to find an anchorage, even if there was one, and it began to appear that another archipelago might have to be passed by with nothing more than a mention in the log. But at the time when Carteret might have turned away to resume the westward course, canoes were observed coming from the largest island making towards the ship and preparations were made to receive them, decks cleared for action, guns loaded and run out, and all hands standing by to repel boarders.

The canoes approaching were seen to be different from those of the Admiralty Isles and came without warlike intent, their crews showing such obvious signs of enthusiasm and friendship that they were immediately allowed aboard, and in a very short time were making the most of their visit talking to the crew in such a friendly fashion, eating and drinking whatever was offered them and then exploring the ship from stem to stern, even going aloft with the confidence and nimbleness of upper yardsmen. Their appearance differed from the islanders previously encountered, more bronze than black, with little beards, long hair similar to the Malay people, and fine white teeth. Their sturdy figures were of medium stature and they went about naked save for a piece of cloth over their privy parts. They had no weapons of any sort and in fact were amazingly friendly and trusting in every way, in Carteret's own words, "merry and familiar with our people as if they had been of long acquaintance." All this left him with the impression that they had previously experienced a visit by a European ship, and a later conversation with one of them appeared to confirm this. Their desire for friendship was sincere, and wishing to make them welcome ashore, they intimated that they would leave one or two of their people on board as a show of good faith. However, they did entertain the idea of trade having brought with them some coconuts for this purpose and had very certain ideas what they wanted in return.

Their particular interest was anything made of iron and were delighted with the offer of nails or pieces of hoop iron from an old cask, in fact they would not trade their coconuts for anything else. Carteret gave one man three pieces of hoop iron, each one no more than four inches long and was quite amazed at the simple pleasure he derived from his acquisition, laughing and jumping for joy, and his fierce reaction when someone tried to take them from him. "Parram! parram!" they kept saying, which had a similar sound to 'parang', the weapon so common amongst the Malays. In the simple language of these islanders it appeared to mean 'iron'.

It was tragic that this one favourable opportunity of friendly relations with native Pacific Islanders from which all hands must have benefited immensely, was frustrated by the poor sailing quality of the *Swallow*. The possibility of reaching the island was receding fast, and yet although the *Swallow*'s distance was increasing all the time, the visitors were in no hurry to leave. In fact one man, who appeared to be at loggerheads with his companions had decided to stay, and no remonstrations from them could induce him to change his mind. Meanwhile, Kerton found time to study the construction of their canoes recording his observations in his log. Although the hull was hewn from a tree-trunk, the sides were raised by planks sewn in place with split cane or something similar. The ends, he noted, were neatly joined and peaked, imparting the hull with a graceful sheer and this, together with the triangular shaped sails, gave them an appearance similar to the rakish proa of the Malays. Their ropes of coconut fibre were well made, their fishing nets also, and their sails were fabricated out of neatly woven pandannus leaves. One characteristic of these craft, which he may have observed but did not mention, is that when going about, they were not tacked through the eye of the wind in the usual way, this being achieved by reversing course and shifting the rudder and sail from one end to the other with the outrigger always to windward.

It was eight bells in the second dog watch before the islanders prepared to leave. The stubborn one refused to go, but many a rough word was exchanged between him and his companions as they prepared to leave. It was a brave decision, coming as he did from his native village to the deck of a warship with strange sights, sounds and smells and a diet of salt beef and hard tack. Carteret, judging that he might be of some use when making friendly overtures at other islands, allowed him to stay. He gave him the name Joseph Freewill, and as such he was duly entered on the ship's muster, no 111, aged 22 and rated A.B. With regard to a name for the archipelago, what could be better than to call it the Joseph Freewill Islands? They remained so until they reverted to their indigenous name as they appear on present day charts, the Mapia Islands, the largest being known as Pegun. Carteret calculated the latitude to be 0° 49'N with a longitude 136° 30'E of Greenwich. The latitude was correct but the longitude was in error by 2° 14' to the west. The two islands to the north, Famedo and Bras were little better than rocks, Carteret wrote, and by what he could see of them he wondered how so many people could find sustenance, and as for water, the inhabitants must survive on rain, the islands being too low for a spring or well. On further reflection he considered that although the inhabitants might welcome future ships, he doubted that they had much to offer in the way of trade.

When the last canoe departed, Carteret, thrusting aside any disappointment he felt at being unable to reach an anchorage and procure fruit and vegetables from the islanders, set the *Swallow*'s course north-west towards the island of Mindanao. Charts of earlier navigators, copies of which he had on board, told him that the Phillipines lay some distance ahead. Dampier, who came this way in 1684, gave a very encouraging account of Mindanao, the southernmost island. "Savannahs abound," he wrote, "with long grass and plentifully stocked with deer. The adjacent woods are a covert for them in the heat of the day, but in the mornings and evenings they feed on the open plains as thick as in the parks of England." On the strength of this from such an eminent explorer and cartographer, Mindanao appeared to be particularly favourable to obtain much needed refreshment.

Carteret had very little to say in his Journal about the next few days. The Celebes lay only 500 miles away and, all being well, another week or two might see the *Swallow* off the coast which held such promise. It could not be too soon for the crew, many of whom, having recovered from scurvy after their spell at English Cove, were once again beginning to suffer from its effects. Progress however was disappointingly slow with the *Swallow* taking four days to cover the next 200 miles.

Chapter XI

On Sunday morning of October 28th, the third day after leaving the Joseph Freewill Islands, Carteret, in order to remind the crew of their duties, read out to them the Articles of War. On the fourth day, the 29th, soon after dawn shoal water was sighted to the north. It was already well abaft the beam when reported and so low-lying that a slight deviation in the course might well have seen the *Swallow* run directly onto it with disastrous consequences. Carteret drew a sketch of its outline in the margin of his log depicting a reef, roughly square-shaped eight or nine miles around the perimeter, encircling a lagoon of smooth water within. He wrote down the position as 2° 53'N 36° 19'E, but as usual his estimate of the longitude was too far to the west by about 4° 1/2'. He considered it exceedingly dangerous, and indeed this was so, being quite invisible on still dark nights, requiring a fresh breeze with the sea breaking over for it to be readily revealed. He named it Bad Man's Shoal and passed on without further investigation. Its name on present day charts is Helens Reef. Kerton noted in his log that four barrels of rainwater were caught that day, proving Carteret's awning was still working well.

Next day, having covered a mere thirty miles since Bad Man's Shoal, an island was sighted from the masthead bearing SW by S about six leagues under the *Swallow*'s lee. There was a fresh breeze blowing from the north-east at the time with heavy rain squalls, and something of a swell running so it was decided not to investigate it further. Because of its particular shape it was given the name of 'Hummock Island'. Yet in spite of the weather a lone canoe was sighted under sail and scudding towards the island now between twenty-five and thirty miles to leewards. It was watched with interest for a while until lost to view when its occupants lowered the sail.

Up until now the current had been mainly in the *Swallow's* favour, helping her along with a westerly set of 1 to 1 and a 1/2 knots, now veered round to the south. The strength was less, not much more than one knot, but the weather, also in her favour for so long, became unsteady with squalls and shifts of direction in the wind frequently catching her aback, splitting the sails and keeping the watch on deck constantly busy with brace and halyard. There were also calms when she lay drifting listlessly with drooping sails for long periods. All this together with her poor sailing qualities found her set to the south, while making no progress at all in the desired direction. Friday, October 5th, was typical of what the *Swallow's* crew had to put up with during this period, and as Kerton's Log tells us:

"At 4 taken aback, braced the yards about and stood to the westward. At half past 5 very hard squall of wind attended with heavy rain. Carried away the larboard main topgallant sheet block which occasioned the sail being blown all to pieces. Shortened sail. At 7 squally with hard rain, wore ship and in first reef. At 8 fresh gale with hard rain. Wore ship and brought to with our head to the southward. At 9 o'clock got down main topgallant yard, unbent the remains of the sail and sent a new one aloft."

Understandably tempers became frayed and seaman James Frazier was flogged this day for insubordination, an unusual event as the "cat" was rarely ordered by Carteret, but Frazier received twelve lashes at the grating for his offence.

This frustrating state of affairs continued for over a week, during which the *Swallow* covered a paltry one oard, spritsail yard, spritsail topsail yard, jibboom and all.

Wednesday brought no abatement, in fact the wind increased even further, a "hard gale" is Carteret's description, this being his strongest term, nothing like adequate under the circumstances. Admiral Beaufort's gradations were still in the future, but 'strong' or 'whole gale', force 9 or 10 on the Beaufort Scale might be nearer the mark, possibly even 11, described as 'storm', with the criterion being "that which would reduce a ship to storm staysails", the *Swallow*'s situation that morning. The stress on the worn out rigging was so great by now that the weaker parts began to give way, the main stay being the first, followed soon after by a chainplate on the larboard fore shrouds. Both of them had straightway to be made good, the former with a tackle set up and hove taut, the latter with a preventer as a makeshift main stay.

Not long after this was done, the leach rope on the main staysail blew out and the sail had to be sent down and repaired. It was time now to reduce the risk of further damage to the tophamper, and accordingly the fore, main and cross-jack yards were lowered almost level with the bulwarks, and then it was the turn of the gaff to come down, followed by the mizzen topsail yard and mizzen topmast itself. Finally, the fore and main topgallant mast were housed; all this done in conditions requiring most outstanding seamanship.

Heavy seas frequently broke on board as she dived into them, flooding the decks: some of this found its way through the seams of the planking, soaking the seamen as they slept in their hammocks and seeping through into the store rooms and sail locker. The hull of the old ship was so badly strained now, that she was leaking to the extent of four feet every watch, and on top of all this, another chainplate broke and the shroud had to be immediately set up again with a tackle before anything else carried away. However, good seamanship and the amazing survival qualities of the ship brought her through the worst of the storm and Thursday found her once again on course for

Mindanao.

But the wind blowing mainly from the south-west bore the *Swallow* steadily northwards, and every effort to coax her to windward met with no success in spite of the southerly set to benefit her. However, on Sunday morning, October 26th, the breeze favoured her on a south-westerly course and she picked up speed.

At dawn, when the crew were aloft setting the topgallants, land was sighted to starboard. The *Swallow* was making better progress now under all sail, with stuns'ls alow and aloft, and as she approached the land, although the weather was hazy at times, mountains were seen in the distance giving Carteret the impression that they were approaching an island to the east of Mindanao, one which was marked on charts in his possession called St Johns, but it was too early to be certain, the estimated distance off at the time being twelve to fourteen leagues.

In the dog watches the following day the *Swallow* encountered calms, squalls, variable winds, even a "sort of tornado", according to an entry in the log. The speed fell away but the southerly set of about two knots helped her on her way southward. The lay of the coast with the mountainous background was deceptive, and at one time it appeared to Carteret to open up into a bay or channel, which he later found did not exist, but as the *Swallow* closed the land, he was able to confirm that it was indeed Mindanao, not the mythical St Johns Island. The weather being fine with good visibility, the countryside could clearly be seen, some of the mountain peaks volcanic, one with smoke issuing from it, while the valleys between were green and forest covered. On Wednesday, October 28th, a point of land was cleared opening up a bay beyond which looked inviting, so the cutter was launched to investigate. Gower was in charge, steering her into the bay while the *Swallow* stood on and off a distance of three miles, waiting for a signal to follow, as there was always a chance that this might be Dampier's Bay of Deer.

It was past midday when the cutter left and she was gone most of the afternoon before a signal was seen from her that the bay was unsuitable. When she arrived back alongside, Gower reported that, at its narrowest part, the depth of the entrance was irregular, only six or seven fathoms, with sand or coral bottom. There were numerous small islets and rocks, and although there may have been good mooring in coves further up, there was insufficient time to investigate. There appeared to be no place to get water and no inhabitants in those parts that he had managed to survey. Altogether, in Gower's opinion, it was not to be recommended, and anyway it certainly was not Dampier's Bay and required no further exploration to confirm this. Carteret's frustration can be sensed by giving it the name Disappointment Bay, and so it remained until it returned to its indigenous name, Pujaga Bay as seen on present day charts.

At noon the following day, Cape St. Augustin bore WSW distant ten miles, and once this headland was passed, there opened up a vast stretch of water, Davao Bay on today's charts, which took up the rest of the day and the following night to cross, a matter of forty miles, slow progress indeed in spite of the favourable current. Mountains at the southern tip of Mindanao were clearly seen at noon on Friday, and later on that day, a distinctive hill or mountain hove in sight fine on the starboard bow in the shape of a sugar-loaf or hummock deemed to be the southern extremity of Mindanao. On approach, however, it was seen to be an island about six miles long, the highest one of a barren archipelago of three with a channel between them and the mainland of five miles.

Sunday, the first day of November, found the *Swallow* rounding Tinaka Point at the southern tip of Mindanao. Carteret now desperately required a port, harbour or coastal city, an outpost of civilisation if possible, where the sick could be treated and the ship repaired. The Dutch and the Spanish were in process of colonising the East Indies, but Batavia and Manila were too far away. Something much nearer was urgently needed. At 2 o'clock that afternoon the cutter was launched to find an anchorage in a bay somewhere with, if possible, a town or village nearby. Lieutenant Gower was in charge as usual and she was away all afternoon, much of the time out of sight from the ship, and, as the evening approached with darkness coming on, there was some apprehension for her on board the *Swallow*, so a 'false fire' – a composition packed into a wooden tube which burnt for several minutes with a blue flame – was burned as a signal for her to return. Soon after this was done, to the relief of all on board the *Swallow*, a similar signal was seen from the cutter. When she came back alongside, Gower had to report that he had found only one anchorage, a small one at that. It lay between two large islands, but there was no sign of inhabitants. Sunday night Carteret kept the *Swallow* standing on and off the coast waiting for daylight. The islands to the south having been found unprofitable, there still remained the southern coast of Mindanao to investigate.

At 7 o'clock next morning Gower took the cutter away, steering a course along the coast to the west of Tinaka Point with the *Swallow* following under easy sail. It was Monday, November 2nd, the day when the first contact with the people of Mindanao was made. The cutter was rounding a point at the time, when a canoe was sighted with a family on board who immediately took fright, paddling away as fast as they could. On reaching the shore they beached the canoe and then fled into the woods taking everything with them. This was a disappointing encounter, but further along the coast another opportunity came, when the cutter entered a little bay which revealed a town, Batulaki (nine miles west of Tinaka Point) within.

However, any expectation of a friendly reception was shattered by the report of a gun, followed soon after by another, but to Gower's relief there was no fall of shot and he concluded that this was a warning either for them or merely alerting the town of an approaching stranger. Which ever it was, three canoes were seen putting to sea, including one particularly large, well-manned one, so Gower decided not to wait to find out their intentions, and turned away to regain the safety of the *Swallow*. The canoes continued the chase until nearing the ship when they abandoned hope of catching up with the cutter and turned away for home.

After such an apparently hostile reception, it was clear to Carteret that the *Swallow* and her crew must fend for themselves without assistance from the local population. Gower was able to acquaint him that he had found a suitable bay a few miles east of Tinaka Point, where there was a safe anchorage with wood and water immediately available. There was really no alternative but to go there, so late that afternoon, the *Swallow* approached the Bay with Gower in the cutter leading the way. At 5 o'clock they came to anchor with the best bower in seven fathoms, after which the cutter carried out the stream anchor for a stern mooring. When this was done the long boat and cutter were immediately sent off for water, the latter being armed and ready for any attack from the shore. There was, however, a fair chance of being left in peace as the nearest inhabitants were three or four leagues away the other side of Tinaka Point.

In the meantime, there were a number of urgent tasks to be carried out aboard the *Swallow*. Some of the running rigging was in a bad state and desperately needed repairing, and there were several worn out sails to be sent down and replaced. While some of the crew attended to this, others were employed rigging a tackle on the mainyard in order to sway four six pounders of the main armament from the hold, stowed below during the long Pacific crossing.

An attack from the shore remained a very real possibility. Also there were well armed proas in these waters ready to prey on any vessel which appeared unable to defend itself adequately. Then the cable, badly worn with so much use, was roused out from the tiers and faked on the deck for inspection and part of it replaced; it was then bent onto the sheet anchor which became the best bower. A spare anchor was hoisted up from the hold which became the sheet anchor.[23]

All this took time, there being forty men on the sicklist with scurvy and unable to take any part in it. But at any rate, there should be no interruptions; the nearest town was four or five leagues to the west on the other side of Tinaka Point. Carteret hoped that the present mooring was remote enough to permit everything to be done without interference. It was a quiet, tree-lined bay with a small river or stream at hand to replenish the casks, and although the water was a trifle brackish to taste, it would serve well enough. There appeared to be no local inhabitants around to interrupt the work. Yet there was some uneasiness on board when later that evening, a small canoe came round the point, remaining for a time studying the situation aboard the *Swallow*. The ensign was hoisted in the hope that they might come and parley, but they would not and left soon after.

No more canoes appeared, neither was there any sign of activity on the shore, and when the boats returned and work ceased for the day, the ship settled down for a restful night at anchor. All was quiet until about 9 o'clock when the peace was shattered, as out of the night came a horrifying shriek from the shores, sudden and hideous, like an Indian war-cry. It was as if a full scale attack was about to be launched and all hands fit enough to do so, stood by to receive it, and although there was relief all round that nothing happened, some of the crew

---

[23] The *Swallow* had three anchors on chess trees at the bow, namely the 'best bower', the one most frequently used, and the 'small bower', in fact 'small in name only as it normally would be of the same weight as the 'best'. The third one, the 'sheet anchor', the largest and heaviest of them would only be used as a last resort on a lee shore. The 'stream anchor' was used as a steadying anchor aft, while the 'kedge' was for warping alongside or 'kedging' up a river. These last two were lighter and handier than the 'bowers' and 'sheet' anchor.

remained on the alert throughout the night.

When daylight came next morning and no sign of activity on the shore, the crew were able to proceed with their work, and soon the guns were coming up from the hold and the anchor cables receiving the attention they so earnestly needed. At eleven that morning, the longboat was sent for water with the cutter in attendance, armed and ready to defend them. Gower was in charge and while the watering was going on, some men came from the wood, one having what appeared to be a white flag which Carteret considered must be a sign of peace. There was no white flag on board the *Swallow* and the best that could be found was a tablecloth. This, when finally exhibited, was accepted and shortly after a man came willingly down to the cutter, and soon after was joined by another. They were both unarmed and greeted the Lieutenant in a very friendly fashion, and although they spoke no English, Gower found that the few words of Dutch and Spanish common between them, enabled him to communicate adequately.

With the help of signs he gathered that the first man was an officer with some sort of authority in dealing with the natives, and that he was interested to find out where the *Swallow* came from, the number of guns she had, and was the Captain a Hollander? He also desired to know whether they had been to Batavia. In this respect he was able to make Gower understand that they should have obtained permission from the local Rajah to sail in these waters, and Gower assured him that this would be done as soon as they had obtained wood and water. During this conversation the man showed admiration for the silk handkerchief Gower had round his neck, and as a gesture of friendship Gower presented it to him, after which the man asked if the ship had anything to trade. Gower assured him of their willingness to do so, but only for provisions. The man replied that if the ship came to the town, she might have as much in the way of provisions as she wanted. Soon after this conversation the two men departed.

On his return to the *Swallow*, Gower reported all this to Carteret. Good relations appeared to have been achieved and the work could now carry on without interruption. A new main topgallant mast was sent up, and while the rigging and sails were having the finishing touches completed, those not involved in these activities were ordered over the side to scrape and clean the strakes between wind and water. At the close of the day the sails and rigging were in as good an order as could at the time be attained: the main armament was in place behind the gunports, anchors and cables overhauled, and the ship in general ready to get under way next morning. The intention was to make a call at the nearby town and then, with fresh supplies on board, set sail for Batavia. There were still a few empty water casks on board so it was decided to fill them while there was time to spare.

As the afternoon wore on, the situation changed with the mood of the people on shore becoming increasingly belligerent. More and more of them could be seen assembling in the wood, posting themselves in groups at different locations, hundreds of them by all account. Some of them kept making sorties onto the foreshore shouting and brandishing their swords in an aggressive and warlike fashion. A few of them were armed with muskets, others, as well as swords, had bows and arrows, spears or pikes and little round shields for hand to hand fighting. On one of their sorties they shot their arrows at the *Swallow*, and blasted off with their muskets in her direction although she was well out of range. However, in spite of all this, there was no mistaking their warning and their determination to repel the seamen should they make any effort to land.

By mid-afternoon the situation became quieter and Carteret sent Gower in the cutter flying the white flag to parley with people, and see if they would allow the longboat to get water. He directed him to approach the shore to a place beyond the range of their arrows and within range of the *Swallow's* six pounders. If necessary, Carteret was prepared to use the guns not only to defend the cutter, but to teach the Mindanaons a lesson. On the other hand, bearing in mind that he intended to call at the town on the other side of Tinaka Point, this was to be avoided if possible.

As the cutter approached the shore, Gower ordered the crew to lay on their oars while he hailed the men hiding in the wood. Not long after, one of them came out to the foreshore and Gower indicated that they had come for water. But the man would not parley, beckoning him to come closer which Gower declined to do. He could see a number of men in the woods beyond. To come closer would bring a hail of arrows down on the cutter with dire consequences. There was to be no watering, that was clear. Ordering the crew to give way together he steered for the *Swallow* to report to Carteret.

Although this incident was not unexpected, Carteret had doubts about the reception the *Swallow* might have at the town beyond Tinaka Point where he intended to call next day. During their stay a number of water casks had been filled, not all of them by any means, but as far as refreshment, anything available ashore had been denied them. He suspected that Dutch influence was behind the antagonism, and the friendly overture at one point was solely an act of spying. For the present however, with the *Swallow's* repairs carried out as well as possible, a restful night at anchor would help set the crew up for whatever the next day might bring.

Chapter XII

Next morning, Thursday, October 5th, preparations were made to clear the anchorage. The weather was cloudy with thunder rumbling and lightning playing around the sky. The breeze, although light, was suitably off-shore for getting under way, and well before dawn the cutter was sent off with orders to help weigh the stream anchor. However, there was a hitch in the proceedings when the buoy rope parted, the anchor being so firmly embedded in the sea bed. This caused some delay while a hawser was bent to the stream anchor cable and when this was done, the capstan was manned and the bower anchor weighed, while paying out the hawser on the stream. The hawser was then taken to the capstan and the stream anchor duly weighed.

By 6.30 the *Swallow* was at last under way. The course was then directed towards Tinaka Point, but while in process of tacking, she missed stays, the breeze being so light requiring the cutter to tow her clear of the bay. After rounding the point she steered for the town. On the approach the weather changed with rain and poor visibility while the breeze chose to veer round to the south, putting the *Swallow* on a lee shore. Furthermore, when within sight of the town, there was no sign of inhabitants, who for some reason kept out of sight, prompting Carteret to abandon his intentions of paying a visit. Thus, hauling his wind, he bore off to the north-west. His best hope now was to locate Dampier's Bay of Deer.

In fact he was closer to it than he realised. The coast beyond the town trended north-west and not long after passing it, a headland, marked on present day charts as Point Siep blit was sighted, beyond which was the entrance to the very bay he was seeking. And yet it did not appear to tally with his perception of it. There were in his cabin copies of all the available charts of this area, some compiled from ancient sources and of little use. The most recent however were Bellin's of 1756, and William Herbert's dated 1758, yet these were of little help, the latitude of the bay being in error and the longitude unreliable. There was also confusion about the Sarangani Islands at the tip of Mindanao, Carteret being led to believe that there were several when in fact there were only two of any size, Balat and Sarangani respectively, the other two being little more than rocks. There were further inaccuracies over Dampier's description of Tinaka Point which he confused with Cape St Augustin.

As the *Swallow* cleared Point Siep blut she was immediately abreast of open water, Sarangani Bay, the indigenous name for Dampier's Bay of Deer where, as Kerton wrote in his log, 'ships might shelter themselves from all winds.' The coast hereabouts was uninhabited, a flat open savannah stretching from the shore to the mountains thirty miles in the distance. The deer were there, just as Dampier wrote, hundreds of them feeding on the plain at night and sheltering in the woodlands during the heat of the day, as much meat as the ship could want, requiring only a reasonable marksman and some able-bodied men to carry the carcasses to the boat. Subsequent navigators were able to confirm this.

Weighing up the situation as it was that day, Carteret made the decision to abandon the search: the lee shore, the inadequacy of his charts and the lateness of the season contributed to this. The hostility of the natives was another factor. With regard to the weather, it remained unsettled with rain and poor visibility, and poor visibility, and having the coast so close under his lee he shaped the *Swallow's* course westward toward more open water.

Native fishing boats were encountered and there was plenty of fish around which it was hoped they might catch some, but with so many canoes everywhere getting in the way and nets becoming fouled the plan had to be abandoned.

Not until November 10th did the wind allow Carteret to turn the *Swallow* on a southerly heading towards the Straits of Macassar, 300 miles to the south-west. He spared no effort to coax a good days run out of the old ship, 83 miles being the best, but often much less, twenty or thirty. There were frequent 'tornadoes', and each time one was encountered, sails had to be swiftly clewed up before they split, but with so many men on the sick list this was not always achieved in time, with consequent damage to sails and rigging.

This situation continued for the next eighteen days. Although the wind was mainly westerly, it varied from NW to SW, keeping the *Swallow* on a bowline most of the time. This required a frequent change of tack in order to maintain a south-westerly course. Being so sluggish in stays, the great sweeps had to be shipped to bring her round when she missed, which she did as like as not. Day followed day with little to mark their passing; on one day a shark weighing 100 lbs was caught, the flesh being shared out among the crew; on another, Seaman James Forrester died of scurvy and was given a sailor's funeral.

December 4th was a particularly hectic one when the *Swallow* encountered a tornado which caught the crew completely unawares. The wind was against the tide at the time, blowing at gale force which brought up a nasty sea, tossing her about unmercifully, frequently breaking on board and flooding the decks. One very harsh squall laid the ship right over on her beam ends, sheets flying, sails thrashing, a nasty situation while it lasted, one which might have seen the last of her had not seamanship prevailed, eventually bringing her back on an even keel and once again on course.

The north-westerly current bore the *Swallow* steadily towards the island of Borneo, the mountains looming up to starboard long before the coast was sighted. There were many inaccuracies in Carteret's charts, not only the coastline, but numerous islands, rocks and sandbanks were laid down where none existed, and others clearly seen but not recorded. Where possible, Carteret made a survey, correcting errors for the benefit of future navigators. On Saturday, November 21st, the islands of Pulo Maratua and Kar Muaras with their dangerous reefs were seen on the starboard hand, and next day the *Swallow* at last entered the Macassar Strait. It was Carteret's desire to take the shortest course down the coast of Borneo but the wind, now blowing consistently from the south-west as she beat way her down, tack after tack, set the *Swallow* over towards the Macassar side while gaining only a few miles southward each day.

November passed into December, and on Thursday, the 3rd, about half way down the Strait she was approaching the 'Paternosters', a string of rocks, islets and shallow sandbanks which extender Macassar, reducing the navigable channel to twenty miles. All this being indifferently charted, the *Swallow* was frequently in danger of running aground on some unseen reef or sandbank, requiring a boat ahead all the time to sound out a clear passage. There were fishermen around and an effort was made to communicate with them but without success, they being too nervous, paddling away as soon as the *Swallow* approached. On Friday, December 10th, she had a brush with a pirate.

The encounter which followed was a lively one raising their spirits and morale just when it was most needed. It commenced bout eight bells in the first dog watch when a large proa was sighted to windward coming up on parallel course. She appeared to have more men on board than warranted for a trading vessel, which made Carteret wary of her intentions. Soon it was seen that she was closing rapidly. Sending the crew to actions stations, muskets were fired to warn her to bear off while at the same time the forecourse was cleared up and headway reduced to allow her to pass ahead if she so desired.

She chose not to, and soon it was apparent that she was not friendly and was coming to board, perhaps being under the impression that the *Swallow* was a helpless merchant ship. As she came close her bulwarks linked with them ready to board, she suddenly opened fire with small canons and muskets, but was speedily disillusioned about her prey by a broadside from the *Swallow*'s starboard main armament, and realising her mistake she immediately tried to bear off in order to pass under the *Swallow*'s stern.

At this, Carteret ordered the helm up, waxing the *Swallow* round to port in time to give her a broadside from the starboard guns. By now the proa knew that she had worthy opponent who was going to maul her severely if she did not immediately break off the engagement and although she had the weather gauge she was unable to do so. Her only means of escaping a further broadside was to repeat her manoeuvre which she did, at the same time keeping up a brisk fire with her little guns and small arms. However, it was of no avail, each time she tried to escape, Carteret was prepared, and although it was dark by now the scene was constantly lit up but the flashes of gunfire, until at last a final well directed broadside from the *Swallow* blew the proa out of the water.

There were no survivors; at least none were picked up, it being too dark to see any. Thus in the end Carteret was unaware of the proa's nationality, but considered that she was a pirate or rover whose crew got their just deserts in the end. The *Swallow* herself came through with no more than her rigging cut up, requiring some knotting and splicing to put it right. Her casualties were two men wounded who were soon patched up by Dr Watson, a seaman being one of them only slightly injured while the other, Lieutenant Gower, had his upper lip creased by a bullet with three of his front teeth damaged.

The high spirits raised during the fight with the pirate soon evaporated. By now there were barely enough men left to work the ship. This, together with the head wind, now that the West Monsoon prevailed, made it unlikely that the *Swallow* would ever reach Batavia. "We were," wrote Carteret in his Journal, "in a sad deplorable situation the sickness was become general nobody on board being free of the scurvy, the current bearing so hard against us that we could neither get westing nor southing." He went on to say that by now all the petty officers were sick leaving only himself and Lieutenant Gower to do the duties normally carried out by these men. Altogether they were in a desperate situation. Fortunately, the Dutch town of Macassar lay 30 miles under the *Swallow*'s lee, a place of some importance being the seat of Government for the island of Celebes, where they could expect to receive a friendlier reception than they did at Butulaki.

His decision to steer for Macassar was an act of desperation, considering the hazards which lay ahead. The approach was beset by a vast area of islets, rocks, reefs and shoals known as the Spermondes, which a vessel without a pilot or local knowledge desiring to approach the harbour must somehow negotiate.

The distance was only thirty miles, but in the end it was to take the *Swallow* three days to reach the harbour. By now, the south-going current had set her thirty miles beyond the latitude of Macassar, and a chart in Carteret's possession appeared to tell him that the best way to get there was to steer an ENE course towards four small islands called the Brothers. These islands lay in a line leading NNW from the island of Tanna Kike off the south-west tip of Celebes, and once clear of them, a course due North would bring the *Swallow* to an anchorage off Macassar.

The coast itself was not yet visible from the ship, although the mountains beyond could be clearly seen. There was the usual debris about, brought down from the rivers, trees and logs, the latter sometimes being mistaken for rocks. The proximity to the coast upset the usually steady West Monsoon causing light breezes from all quarters with the *Swallow* boxing the compass and making little progress. When, however, the sea breeze took over at an hour before noon as it did each day, she was able to take advantage of this while it lasted. Very soon she was among the shoals proceeding under all sail, royals and stuns'ls and a seaman in the chains with the lead going all the time.

In spite of every effort to steer a straight course towards the Brothers, an undetected current bore the *Swallow* northward, and on Sunday morning about noon she grounded on a shoal called The Thumb. A previous cast of the lead had given four fathoms but shoaling, and before another cast could be taken she grounded. Her draught at the time was around eleven feet, or a little more according to her trim, but she was soon coaxed off into deeper water again without any damage. She continued this way for the next three days with the cutter leading the way, manned by the healthiest members of the crew, the only ones sufficiently able to ply an oar. Soundings were taken as she went for the deeper water and sometimes, when there was no breeze, she carried the kedge anchor out while those on board capable of doing so, manned the capstan to heave the ship ahead. At night the ship was brought to anchor while the crew rested, gathering strength for an equally arduous time next day. Hours later, when at dawn the ship came to life again, those on deck found the ship surrounded by fishing boats busy with their lines and nets. They tried to make contact with them, sending the cutter over hoping to purchase some fish, but they appeared to be frightened and made off without waiting.

At 11 a.m., when the sea breeze commenced to blow, the anchor was weighed and sail made. A number of posts were sighted to which fishermen attached their lines and nets, and also appeared to mark a channel leading towards the town. At 4 a.m., a small fort hove in sight with the Dutch flag flying over it, a sign that the *Swallow* had at last reached civilisation. Hoisting her ensign, she continued her approach until the breeze failed at 7 p.m. when she was brought up with the stream anchor, 246 days from the Straits of Magellan and 1 year, 3 months and 25 days since her departure from Plymouth. It was December 16th, one day having to be added for crossing the 180th Meridian.

If Carteret had expected a welcome from the authorities, he was disappointed. The Dutch, like the colonisers of the eastern dominions, particularly the Spanish and Portuguese, guarded their territories with dogged resistance, taking exception to vessels belonging to other nations. The gold, silver and spices of the islands were too precious to share with others. Macassar was an important centre of trade in the region with a garrison manning the fort known as Castle Rotterdam for its defence. It was the key to the Spice Islands, 600 miles to the east and the policy of the Dutch Authorities and the Dutch East India Company was to deny ships of other nations the opportunity to trade in these waters. Relations with local kings and princes were tenuous, and foreign ships could foment trouble between them and the Dutch.

The anchor was not long down before a Dutch official paid the *Swallow* a visit, albeit a very peremptory one. His name was Jacobus Heere, a naval overseer. The *Swallow*'s arrival had been reported a long time before she came to anchor, early enough for the Macassar Council to call a meeting, which when convened, decided that until the purpose of the strange vessel was made known, no members of the crew should be allowed ashore. After all, such a weather-worn vessel might be a pirate, even though she was flying the flag of a nation known to be at peace with the Government of the Netherlands. Heere was nervous about boarding a strange vessel, and even more concerned when he learnt there was sickness aboard and forthwith declined to go below; scurvy was a common complaint at this time, soon to be eradicated from the nautical world, but other serious diseases could be found aboard any ship, and smallpox in particular could ravage a community having no natural immunity to it.

Nonetheless, at daylight next morning Carteret sent Lieutenant Gower in the cutter with a letter to the Governor acquainting him of the reason for the *Swallow*'s visit, and at the same time requesting the liberty to get fresh food and stores for the crew. He further desired a sheltered berth or anchorage for the ship, and permission to remain until the change of the Monsoon.

For Gower and the cutter's crew it was a most unrewarding day. The Lieutenant's instructions from Carteret were explicit: he must deliver his message to the Governor only or at any rate his immediate representative, in order to get the attention the ship and the crew so desperately needed. In all fairness to Gower, he did his best only to meet with a complete lack of goodwill or co-operation.

When the cutter reached the wharf, he nor any of the crew were allowed ashore, nor was any person or boat allowed to approach or communicate with them in any way. For the next four hours they waited in the hot sun with no shelter and seemingly no prospect of delivering the letter to the Governor. During this long and tedious wait, Gower could see evidence of two vessels, sloops he called them, although one of them was only a native proa adapted for the purpose, either as a defence against the *Swallow* if she should attack, or preparations to launch an attack on the ship herself. Eventually he managed to give his letter to a man whom he took to be the Harbour Master, known as the Shabandar in those parts.

Back on board the *Swallow*, Carteret, anxious for a reply, was preparing to weigh anchor since there was no sign of any official paying a visit. He intended to take her to a berth closer to the town while the sea breeze lasted. This he was unable to do without the cutter's crew to help man the capstan, they being the healthiest and strongest in the ship. With all hands so desperate for fresh food, this delay in procuring it was frustrating beyond measure.

At 11 a.m. Gower returned with the message that two men would come to the *Swallow* in due course to find the purpose of her voyage and deliver her orders from the Governor. He informed Carteret that he had been prevented from delivering the letter personally to the Governor, whom he been told was sick; but someone would come out later.

They came eventually, two people, a soldier and a writer of the Dutch East India Company. They were of no importance, merely minor officials, the soldier, Le Cerff by name, an ensign of the local garrison, the writer, Abraham Douglas, the son of a Scotsman. It turned out that neither of these two could speak English, not even the Scottish writer. However, the ensign was French, so the contents of the letter were translated into French, the language common to all three of them. It was quite clear: the *Swallow* must leave instantly; must not approach the town; neither anchor on any part of the coast, nor allow anyone to go ashore.

Carteret had no thought of agreeing to such demands, re-affirming the dire condition of the *Swallow* and her crew. He had made this quite clear in his letter. He stressed to the two men that it should be understood that this was no way to treat a ship of His Britannic Majesty's Navy on a peaceful mission, entering a port which flew the flag of Holland, which he deemed to be a friendly country. He reminded them of this and that their two nations were signatory to a Treaty of Friendship which bound them to give assistance to any of His Majesty's ships which entered their waters.

The Governor, David Boelen, had come out from Holland a bare four months previously and should certainly have been aware of the Treaty, but pressure from the Dutch East India Company, who made every effort to keep foreigners from trading in their rich territories, may have influenced him to ignore it. This was a vastly different welcome from the friendly reception Carteret had experienced two years ago in the Dutch port of Batavia when he came there in the *Dolphin* in 1765 with Commodore Byron.

Carteret's remonstrations with his two visitors over the injustice that was being done to a King's ship, one so desperately in need, had a great effect on them, particularly when they were shown numbers of the crew so sick and emaciated. But in spite of all his reasoning with them, he was unable to make them change their minds and give him permission to bring the ship close to the town. Becoming quite frustrated at this lack of good will, he threatened forthwith to sail in and anchor close under the walls as a protest against the disgraceful welcome they had received. On hearing this, the Ensign begged him not to. He must wait until he heard from the Governor again. Neither he nor Douglas had the authority to give permission to come nearer the town. There might be better news when they returned ashore with their report of the *Swallow*'s condition. In the end Carteret agreed to this: he was impressed by the courtesy of these two men, Douglas in particular, who informed him that there was a great deal of sympathy in the town, especially the ladies when they learnt of the *Swallow*'s desperate needs. He told them he would wait a while longer but only until next morning, when as soon as the sea breeze commenced he intended to sail in, regardless of their protests and the undying shame of Governor Boelen's orders. Eventually the two men left, taking with them a second letter to deliver to the Governor.

At 6 o'clock next morning one of the proas seen by Gower being armed the previous day, came up with the land breeze, anchoring close on the *Swallow's* starboard bow. Kerton noted in his log that she had four carriage guns, six swivels and a crew of twenty men, no great threat, but a short while later the second guard boat appeared, taking up a mooring close on the *Swallow's* larboard bow. She was described by Kerton as a sloop, armed with six carriage guns and ten swivels and a larger complement of men than the proa, forty in all. The question was, were the two of them there to attack the *Swallow*, after dark perhaps, or merely to discourage the crew from moving her closer to the town? Time would tell, but at any rate Carteret was not to be discouraged by them and gave orders for the cable to be hove short. He also sent Gower over in the cutter to inquire their intentions but they would not allow him to come alongside.

Then, if anything was needed to determine him to carry out his intentions, Seaman Edward Wheatly died of scurvy that morning. If nothing was achieved immediately to obtain fresh food, more deaths would follow.

When at around midday the sea breeze commenced, the capstan was manned. As the anchor came home, Carteret watched the sloops anxiously while the *Swallow's* sails were sheeted home. If they made any effort to oppose him, he was prepared to fight, broadside to broadside if necessary, but to his relief they made no threatening moves, only weighing their anchors and following slowly in his wake. Anyway his attention was soon diverted by the sound of music coming from a handsome craft approaching from the direction of the town with a number of gentlemen on board and a small orchestra.

When this craft was within hailing distance they made Carteret understand that they had a letter from the Governor, but would not come aboard unless the ship came to anchor. This was done immediately, and as soon as the *Swallow* was brought up, the boat came alongside and delivered on board the Shabander, Jan Hendrik Voll, who was Chief Officer of the port, also the Fiscal, Frederick van Blizdenberg, an officer of the Customs, and other Dutch officials including Abraham Douglas, the previously mentioned writer of the Dutch East India Company. There were also a number of local merchants who had come along for the ride. Altogether, with the music, it was quite a jolly party and they were ushered into the grand cabin where they were courteously invited to be seated.

Relations were somewhat strained at first, particularly when the Shabander expressed surprise that they had found the *Swallow* under sail as they approached, to which Carteret answered that yesterday, he had informed Ensign Le Cerff and Mr Douglas that he would come in on the morrow about midday, when the sea breeze commenced if he had not received a reply to his letter to the Governor. This he had done, having not been favoured with a reply. He pointed out that their most pressing needs dictated this, and protested against the casual and indeed unfriendly way his ship, a vessel of the British Royal Navy, obviously in distress, was being treated by the authorities in Macassar. Did they not know that Holland and Britain were at peace? The situation on board, as they could well see, with a sick crew and leaking ship, was so desperate that he was prepared to run the ship ashore under the walls of the city, and if fired upon, to sell their lives dearly since they would all perish shortly anyway for want of nothing more than the good will expected of a friendly country.

All this was listened to with great patience and forbearance, excusing their lateness in coming out to him. The Macassar Council met at 8 o'clock that morning, they told him, and they had hurried out as soon as the Governor's letter had been written. As a gesture of good will they had brought something for the ship's immediate needs, namely two sheep, an elk, some fowls, vegetables and fruit. These were received with sincere thanks and sent to the galley right away. They also brought the letter from the Governor in reply to Carteret's of the day before. This, in fact, was no different from the previous one ordering him to depart immediately. The reason for this stern measure was blamed on pressure from the Dutch East India Company and local Kings and Princes, who forbade them to allow ships of any nation, other than the Dutch, to trade or even visit these parts. The letter made no allowance for the difference between a merchant ship and a naval vessel, and it was of the first importance to show them around the ship to convince them that the *Swallow* was not one of the former.

The visitors were soon aware that the condition of the ship and her crew was as bad as Carteret had made out, and that under the circumstances she urgently required assistance if she were to survive the South-West Monsoon. There were sick men in the lower deck in large numbers, fifty of them at least, infected with scurvy to such a degree that most had loose teeth, swollen gums and were unable to walk, let alone perform any duties. They were also shown the body of Seaman Wheatly to further convince them, and having seen all this, they were taken to the hold where they found nothing more than a few barrels of ship's stores. Of water, only the ground tier remained and with regard to food, there was a cask of dried peas, two of salt pork and four of beef. There were half a dozen casks of oatmeal and one of flour remaining, while three hogshead of brandy just about completed the stores apart from the hard tack in the bread room aft. The boatswain's and carpenter's store rooms were inspected and having seen all this, they returned to the Grand Cabin where Gower opened up a hatch in the after end beneath the stern windows, revealing the bread room. It was almost empty, barely two months hard tack remaining and like every other compartment they had inspected, completely void of anything resembling cargo or contraband.

Yet even after all this, the visitors remained unconvinced and further discussions followed during which Carteret reminded them that he had visited these parts two years previously in His Britannic Majesty's ship *Dolphin*, coming to anchor at Batavia where he had been given all possible convenience and facilities without any protest. Why was the *Swallow* being treated in such a cavalier fashion in Macassar?

Their reply was unequivocal. They would appear foolish, they said, to allow ships of any nation, either private or man-of-war into these waters without genuine proof provided beforehand. Mere assertions were insufficient, they insisted.

When this was translated to him by Douglas, Carteret became overwhelmed with emotion. All the evidence was there, he told them heatedly, a ship of the British Royal Navy in dire distress, seeking only shelter and assistance from a nation, supposedly friendly, which by treaty was honour bound to give them. They must bear in mind that the crew was so incapacitated, so weak that they were only able to handle the smallest anchor, leaving the ship in danger of dragging ashore in any sort of a strong wind. In their approach to the port they had run aground on the Thumb and the ship was leaking[24]. Furthermore, what was the reason for sending two armed vessels to anchor so close in such a threatening manner?

At this show of anger and frustration having been so blatantly mistrusted, the visitors began to appreciate the problems facing Carteret and became more reasonable. They assured him it was pressure from native potentates which required them to ensure that visiting ships of countries other than the Dutch were discouraged; the Governor's letter made this quite clear. They were conscious of his needs, very pressing indeed (the ship was leaking, as Carteret said, but this was not caused by the grounding on the Thumb, but as a result of earlier damage to the bow), they could not dispute that, but they would like to be made aware of from whence he had come and on what territories he had landed. They also required to know the true purpose of the voyage. Once they had received knowledge of all this, arrangements could be made for the well-being of both ship and crew. With regard to the two armed ships he referred to, they were posted there purely for his own protection against Malay thieves or pirates.

Somewhat mollified by this, although not by any means believing their explanation for the two ships, Carteret produced his Commission. This confirmed his authority to command the *Swallow*, and was proof of her being a warship of His Britannic Majesty's Navy. It was an impressive document embellished with anchors and crossed cannons, signed by several people including Lord Egmont, then First Lord of the Admiralty, Sir

---

[24] The ship was leaking, as Carteret said, but this was not caused by the grounding on the 'thumb' but as a result of earlier damage to the bow.

Charles Saunders who followed him, and Augustus Keppel, who also became First Lord some years later. Philip Stevens, the Admiralty Secretary had added his signature to the document. However this did not seem to impress the visitors greatly who appeared surprised that it was written in English. What did they expect? Latin perhaps which they could translate more readily? However, they had great interest in the charts, and one of the company remarked that on such a long voyage there must needs be a mort of paper work, log books and journals etcetera and this indeed was the case, there being what amounted to four quires in total. A study of the relevant charts and logs revealed that the ship had not touched at the Moluccas, nor as far as they could ascertain, any other of the Spice Islands.

The visitors were at last convinced that the *Swallow* was not a merchant vessel but a warship of a friendly nation, and that she was certainly very much in distress with her sickly crew, and in danger of ending up on a lee shore if caught in a gale. They noted that the standing and running rigging was worn and bleached quite white, while the hull, at least what they could see of it below the waterline, was green with long fronds of weed. They also observed that the general condition of the ship, as far as cleanliness was concerned, left much to be desired. They counted the guns of the main armament to include in their report to the Governor, together with swivels and muskets.

Having completed their investigation their attitude became friendlier, and Carteret at last was aware of this, However they told him that it was not in their power to permit the ship to stay in Macassar nor allow any of the crew ashore. They were sympathetic to his needs, and indeed there was sympathy by people in the town because of the harsh treatment they were receiving from the council. However, they had an alternative to offer which he might consider.

There was, down the coast, a suitable berth at a place called Bonthain Bay which offered good shelter from the South-West Monsoon where the *Swallow* could lie at anchor, The sick men could go ashore where a hospital might be set up in which they might recuperate. Supplies for their refreshment would be sent there from Macassar. They could remain there until the change of the Monsoon when, with the ship and crew once more in good order, they could proceed on their way. A pilot would assist with the navigation round the coast to the anchorage. There was a small fort there for their protection, and the resident in charge of the small settlement by name of Sergius Swellengrebel had English connections and would look after their interests and arrange for supplies, which of course would have to be paid for. Much of this was indeed welcome. The Shabander and his associates were throwing Carteret a lifeline, and he grasped it immediately. But cautious as ever, he requested that all this might be confirmed in an official letter which should include a declaration that the *Swallow* and her crew would be under the protection of the Dutch Government, and that there would be an end to any threat to the ship or her people. They assured him that it would be so, and gave him their word of honour.

At last it was time for them to leave. The visit had been successful on both sides, even the matter of paying the *Swallow's* bills had been agreed. With regard to the supplies, Carteret offered to pay for them, but this was politely declined, and when they departed, they took with them a present from him to the Governor of a dozen bottles of Madeira and half an English cheese, not a great gift but most probably the best which the *Swallow* could provide at the time. Then, as a final gesture of good will, Carteret ordered a salute of nine guns to be fired in their honour, that being the same for an admiral in terms of naval etiquette.

It now appeared that all was settled and that the *Swallow* would soon be safe in a sheltered mooring. Although Carteret had never visited Bonthain Bay, records in his possession described it as a suitable haven at the time of the South-West Monsoon. It was Saturday, December 19th. Sunday should see the *Swallow* on her way there.

Chapter XIII

Dawn the following day found the *Swallow* still at anchor with no immediate signs of preparation to get under weigh. As it turned out, with no particular need to hurry, another twenty-four hours elapsed before she did. Although ready in all respects to proceed to Bonthain, the written order from the Governor had not been received, and Carteret had no intention of sailing until it came, together with the assurance that the *Swallow* would continue under the protection of the Dutch Government. Relations between the *Swallow* and the authorities in Macassar had improved although a visit from the Shabander the previous evening, upset Carteret considerably when he was informed that there was no money available from the council to give him credit, nor any in the chest of the Dutch East India Company. "It was their entire fault," he told the Shabander indignantly. All this trouble could have been avoided if he had been allowed ashore to negotiate credit. It was as if they had been prisoners or enemies even, instead of friends. He would have been prepared to pay for their food, which by international law and even common decency; it was their duty to supply.

The Shabander assured him that there was no need to worry. The Resident for the Dutch Authorities at Bonthain, Sergius Swellengrebel by name, had English connections. He would supply the *Swallow* with everything she required. He was a man of property in England, married to an English lady. Payment could be arranged through him. Once the *Swallow* was anchored at Bonthain, he could have a hospital for the sick. He would find that refreshments were more plentiful there, and whatever else the ship required, would be sent from Macassar. Of course, everything received must be paid for.

In spite of the Shabander's assurance that everything was being done for the benefit of the ship and crew, Carteret considered it to be the reverse. The presence of the guardships, the denial of any contact with the populace, the banishment of the ship to a remote bay did not add up to the actions of one friendly nation towards another. However, since for the present there was nothing he could do to alter the situation, it behoved him to comply with their wishes. In his present mood of suspicion he made it clear to the Shabander that, if there was any foul play, they would answer for all the consequences.

Affairs began to move in the evening when Ensign Le Cerff came aboard accompanied by the Secretary of the Macassar Council, Meneer Joseph Smoder, who brought two letters with him, one for Carteret, the other for the Resident at Bonthain. When he read his own letter he found that it differed very little from the others, being full of restrictions, and in his own words, "a manifest contradiction of the 'Treaty of Friendship and Alliance' subsisting between our two nations." He increasingly began to consider that the authorities were deliberately deceiving him, particularly when he observed the two guardships embarking additional soldiers. At the sight of these he demanded to see the contents of the letter to the Resident.

The addition to the guardships of two sergeants, two corporals and thirty-six privates pointed towards even more restrictions for the *Swallow*'s crew. This was so, as he found out, when he was finally allowed to read the Resident's letter. No one was to be allowed ashore apart from the sick, nor given the opportunity to communicate with other ships or boats which might try to come alongside. The sick, however, would be allowed to find shelter in a hospital ashore, and the Captain would be permitted to disembark and stretch his legs, if he so desired, but only after making a request to the Resident. With regard to the two armed vessels, they were to accompany the *Swallow* round to Bonthain Bay and take up their moorings close to her to discourage any contact with other craft. The suggestion was that this should be considered a favour. In order to make further communication even more difficult, all French or English speaking people in Bonthain were to be packed off to Macassar out of the way.

With all these restrictions it was no wonder that Carteret felt that he was being treated in a most unfriendly way, resulting in his attitude becoming somewhat truculent. The Dutch Authorities on their part considered that he lacked gratitude for the favour they had bestowed on him.

On Sunday, after a quiet night, all hands were called, and those able to do so manned the capstan to weigh anchor. It was 5 o'clock, not yet daylight when the *Swallow* was brought under sail steering a southerly course with a light breeze to help her along. By 9 o'clock she passed the little island of Glisson to port, and from there shaped a course to pass between the mainland and the island of Tanakiki with the two guardships following in her wake. They had no trouble in keeping up with the *Swallow* as her speed rarely exceeded three knots. Midmorning found her abreast of the Three Brothers, and by noon she had only just passed Tanakiki Island. The breeze now picked up and with it her speed, almost 5 knots at times. In spite of this, as the afternoon drew on, it was apparent to the pilot that she would not reach Bonthain before dark, so just after sunset he brought her to anchor with the stream under the lee of Cape Boele to the west.

At 6 o'clock next morning, under the orders of the pilot, sail was made for the last leg to a mooring at the top of the Bay. At 11 a.m. the *Swallow*, after a slow passage up, was brought to anchor with the small bower about three quarters of a mile from the shore. To the north lay the town of Bonthain situated at the mouth of a little river where there was a small fort of eight guns nearby for its protection. As the *Swallow* made her approach, she saluted the fort with eleven guns which duly answered with the same number.

It was Tuesday, December 22nd, when Carteret set about mooring the *Swallow* as safely as possible. He ordered the cutter and the longboat to be launched, intending to carry out the stream anchor towards the shore with a long scope of cable in order to warp the ship closer in. When this was done she was moored with both bower anchors, one to the north, the other to the south with a cable on each so as to have, as Carteret wrote in his log, "open hawse to the NW and SW." As soon as the *Swallow* was brought up at her mooring the two guard ships sailed up and came to anchor nearby.

Although the situation was far from friendly with all the restrictions involved, at least it was a safe anchorage, well protected from the North East Monsoon. Away from the little town the coast was forested and would supply all the wood required for the *Swallow's* galley, and the water casks could be filled without too much trouble from the river. It was a busy anchorage with numerous vessels coming and going, others anchored waiting for a let up in the Monsoon to allow them to proceed westward. Most were native proas, trading or fishing craft, except a few Dutch vessels making for the Spice Islands or returning homewards loaded. It was much frequented by proas fishing for beche-de-mer, a kind of sea slug, a delicacy in China and so much in demand that sometimes there were as many as a hundred of these craft in this trade, fishing the waters round the islands. Meanwhile, the *Swallow* was being prepared for a long stay: the sails were loosed and left hanging to dry before being unbent and stowed below; and when this was done, it was the turn of the topgallant yards to come down; the spritsail yard was also unrigged and stowed in the booms alongside the topgallant yards.

Christmas Day passed in the same way as any other day of the week, much of it occupied in sending down the topgallant yards and masts, and unreeving the running rigging to be stowed down below. In the meantime Carteret ventured ashore to wait on the Resident in order to make provisions for the sick. The Resident, Sergius Swellengrabel, spoke very little English but was as helpful as he was permitted to be by the Dutch Authorities in Macassar. He made a house available situated near the fort, to which twenty-five sick seamen were brought, those that were so ill and considered by Doctor Watson unlikely to recover in the close confines of the *Swallow's* tween deck. Fresh stores began to arrive, a mixed bag consisting of two fawns, one elk and a hog together with some groceries including rice. Also included was tobacco and six barrels of arrack, the local drink made from rice which would take the place of rum. With all this in hand, the crew were put on their full rations again, and although the quality of the food gave nothing to complain about, Carteret considered the prices quite unreasonably high.

Meanwhile trouble was brewing on the *Swallow* with the dread word 'mutiny' appearing in the log, The 'people', as the men before the mast were referred to, who during the voyage had been so loyal, now began to show signs of unrest, not surprising after so long a period with no immediate prospect of a jaunt ashore.

The first sign was when Seaman James Shaughnessy was found to be drunk on duty, having obtained rum or arrack from the sickbay not consumed by the patients. He received twelve lashes of the 'cat' for this, and for a day or two there were no other incidents with the two ship's boats kept busy, the long boat going up the river for fresh water strictly guarded by soldiers, while the cutter, under Lieutenant Gower's direction, went fishing with the seine. Permission had to be sought from the Resident for this and was duly granted, but the result of two days with the net was a catch of only a few small fish. After such poor returns the fishing was abandoned and the following morning the wood cutting resumed.

It was New Year's Eve. The boats set off soon after dawn for wood, and as usual, the shore party was met by soldiers who guarded them but not the cutter. In the meantime, those left to tend the moorings managed to buy a quantity of arrack from local inhabitants. This they hid and later conveyed back to the ship, together with the firewood, and smuggled it on board. During the forenoon watch the wind freshened from the southwest with no boatwork possible until at one bell in the first dog watch, the weather improved and Gower ordered the cutter away to see if the fresh meat for the ship had arrived. As the boat's crew assembled they were found mostly to be drunk, including Ross, the coxswain. Gower tried to assemble another crew, but of the few seamen fit enough to ply an oar, most were also drunk. One exemption was Seaman Hollis who appeared sober, but was impertinent, even mutinous when ordered to go into the boat. At this Gower directed all those who had been drinking to repair aft to the quarter-deck, and having seen to this, he then went below to inform the Captain that the crew were in a state of mutiny.

Under normal circumstances the Marines would have been called out to restore order, but this was not done, in fact they are not mentioned in the log, being no doubt numbered among the sick. However, those of the afterguard stood by Carteret when he came on deck and soon restored a semblance of order. Hollis continued to be the most outspoken, complaining about grievances long past, even going back to Mas Afuera. He had no support from his shipmates except Ross, and eventually these two were put in irons. Then the ship was searched for liquor, none being found having already been consumed.

All this was the result of too much leniency, wrote Kerton in his log, some truth perhaps but the *Swallow* was not a ship ruled by the 'cat', although there were occasions when it was needed for discipline to be maintained. And now was the time to use it to discourage any further drunkenness and acts of mutiny. Carteret considered a court martial, but the delay required in assembling one forbad this. So next day, all hands were assembled on deck to hear the Articles of War read out to remind them of the dire penalties for drunkenness and mutiny, and when this was done, the grating was rigged. First Hollis, then Ross were lashed to the grating to receive their punishment, one dozen strokes of the 'cat' for the former and two dozen for the latter.

It was a much depleted crew assembled on the quarter-deck to witness the punishment, with twenty-five men ashore in the hospital, and others confined to the sickbay on board. But from now on conditions improved, albeit slowly. The crew soon settled down to the routine; rest, improved feeding, light but regular duties combined to bring most of them back to health. William Sennet, boatswain's mate, an unusually bad case of scurvy, confined to his hammock for the best part of six months, was now at last getting better and able to go ashore to the hospital. Sadly, scurvy still took its toll with one of the carpenter's mates succumbing to it, a sad loss, as the *Swallow's* tradesmen were particularly needed for the repairs.

With the prospect of four months ahead before the beginning of the South-West Monsoon, there was time enough to improve the *Swallow's* condition. Even at anchor she was still leaking badly, but little could be done to the hull in this direction except caulk the decks and sides above the waterline. At least the spars and rigging could be attended to and while this was being done, the main yard was found to be badly sprung, and with no forge on board they would have to make shift with it until Batavia. And now, just when affairs appeared to be going satisfactorily, there was an occurrence which caused Carteret particular concern.

One day towards the end of March, when the cutter was ashore fetching stores, a man handed Gower a letter. The bearer, a coloured man, after delivering it departed as discreetly as he came. The letter was addressed to "The Commander of the English Ship," and appeared to be intended for the *Swallow*, so on his return to the ship, Gower gave it to Carteret. It contained more disturbing news.

When Carteret read the letter, he found that it gave a dire warning of intrigue and treachery. A gentleman by the name of Nicholas Ray was the author. He wrote giving warning that the King of Boni, whose realm lay to the south, was about to make an attempt to capture the *Swallow*. He went as far as to say that the King of Boni's son, with 800 men under his command, was to lead the attack. The Dutch would supply powder and shot, and the King's son would receive a present from them and have the plunder from the ship. Mr Ray's advice was to be particularly wary of approaches by people who appeared to be friends, with offers of slave girls, or provisions in the form of cattle, fowl or fruit, all with the intention of lulling the ship into a state of false security. The Dutch wrote Ray, pretended that they had no part in this, which was not the case. He himself had got wind of the plot from King Aron Matoa of the Buginese, whose realm adjoined the kingdom of Boni. Mr Ray was quite adamant that all this was true: "These black villains stick at nothing to complete their ends," he said, adding that he hoped to visit the ship shortly to give more information.

When Carteret read the letter he was taken by surprise. The Dutch, although far from friendly, were not threatening. At least he had seen no clear indications that they might attack the *Swallow*. That one of the local kings might do so was something he could expect, piracy being a way of life in these islands, but the Dutch having a hand in it was something of a surprise. And yet, when he considered the matter carefully, certain recent occurrences began to make him suspicious. One in particular was the presence of a canoe, frequently observed by the watch during the night, paddling quietly around the ship as if to see whether the crew were on the alert. Then there was the withdrawal of the guard ship, a large, well-manned sloop, which, in addition to the crew, mustered two army officers and a platoon of soldiers, there for his protection he had been told, so why was it no longer necessary? Furthermore, there was the appearance of a troop of soldiers which Carteret was given to understood was intended for an expedition to Bali, but who was to say that this was not merely a cover up for something more sinister? Clearly it was his duty to be on guard and ready for any attack which might come.

He immediately set about preparing the ship for such an eventuality. After informing Gower of the threat, he ordered all the guns of the main armament to be loaded, also the swivel guns on the fore part of the quarter-deck, four in number. When this was done, the sails previously brought down for repair were sent aloft and bent, while the moorings were prepared ready to get under weigh at a moment's notice. During the night watches all hands lay under arms, with cutlass and loaded musket at their side, and any boarders were likely to get a hot reception. From now on the *Swallow* continued under a state of siege and imminent attack, but being warned of it, Carteret relished the thought of action, being quite certain that ship and crew "would have given a good account of double the number if they had come."

In the end there was no attack, although the threat of one persisted. Ensign Le Cerff was in command of the troop. He came to see Carteret, a courtesy visit he assured him. Looking around the decks he could not fail to notice the loaded guns, the burning matches, the primed muskets with bayonets fixed, in fact everything in train ready to repel boarders. He remarked on this, and after hearing the reasons for the situation on board, he did his best to allay his fears. Carteret however, always suspicious of anything concerning the Dutch Authorities, rebuffed the friendly approach, assuming that the intention of the visit was to learn the present ability of the ship and crew to defend themselves, all of which he implied in so many words.

At this, Le Cerff protested most strongly that he had neither knowledge nor any part in such plans to capture the ship: he was a man of honour, he insisted, and with Carteret's attitude as it was, he might well have demanded satisfaction.

However, good sense on the part of the Ensign prevailed and a duel was avoided. He did his best to allay Carteret's apprehensions, and quite naturally requested to know where the information of the suspected attack came from. This Carteret was not prepared to divulge, only going as far as to admit that a letter had come to hand with the warning. He reminded the Ensign of a previous incident of Dutch intransigence when an English ship was attacked a few years previously in similar circumstances at nearby Amboina.

With great patience Le Cerff assured him that the *Swallow* was safe under the Macassar Council's protection. Had he not been well treated since he came to these parts? He requested to see the letter to learn the name of the bearer of such unreasonable accusations, and although Carteret had a high opinion of Le Cerff, he was unwilling to reveal any further information in spite of being mollified by the Ensign's assurances. He trusted Le Cerff, and was prepared to admit that in many respects the *Swallow* had been well treated. At last, when the Ensign left, the two men parted on good terms, although on Carteret's part he was not completely convinced of Dutch good faith, and kept the crew on the alert just the same. Meanwhile he tried to get in touch with Swellengrabel, only to find that he was not around, being up country on business, and this gave him some concern: had he been sent away deliberately, having no part in the conspiracy? Carteret trusted the Resident, considering it unlikely that he would. He was expected back next day, April 1st, but when he did not return his suspicions increased, so he sent a letter to him demanding to see him forthwith. His failure to return immediately did nothing to allay Carteret's fears.

When Swellengrabel returned the following day, on learning about the supposed attack, he did his best to persuade Carteret that there was no basis for the rumour, at least not where the Dutch Authorities were concerned. Could he not be told the name of the informant? To his credit Carteret declined to put Ray in any way at risk. This left little for Swellengrabel to go on, and the only possible way to obtain reliable information was to send spies into the Kingdom of Boni. There, they might be able to ferret out how far advanced such plans were, even if they existed at all. It was Carteret's desire that this should be done immediately, and Swellengrabel agreed.

The days passed with the spies having little success. What they did find out failed to pin-point any immediate danger. An envoy of the King of Boni paid the Resident a visit with the most trifling excuse, which immediately gave grounds for suspicion; and there was also a report that a Boni Prince had been visiting Bonthain in spite of every effort to keep this secret. It appeared that both these missions had the intention of spying out the situation with regard to the *Swallow's* defences. More important to the Dutch Authorities was information from their spies reaching them about an Englishman in the region suspected of encouraging dissent among the Buginese.

The King of the Bugi was no friend of the Dutch: his Kingdom lay on the other side of the Straits of Malacca in the south-eastern part of Borneo where the Dutch held no sway. In spite of this they restricted his trade to such an extent that he had turned to piracy in those waters. The Dutch in return, when they captured any Buginese proas, treated their crews without mercy, according to Carteret's Journal, sometimes chopping off their arms and legs before throwing them bodily overboard to the sharks; others more fortunate in their treatment were sold into slavery. When it became known to the King that an English warship was in Bonthain, he sent Ray to make contact with the Captain offering a safe refuge, if needed. In return he hoped that the *Swallow* might help him regain control of the waters around his coast.

It was no great surprise to Carteret when Ray paid the *Swallow* a visit. He appeared at the hospital on Monday, May 18th, where he discreetly introduced himself having crossed the Straits of Malacca in a local proa. From the hospital he was directed to the ship. He succeeded in passing quite unnoticed by the Authorities, being dressed in English clothes and taken for one of the crew. When at last the two men came face to face in the Grand Cabin, Carteret found him to be a pleasant young man, a writer by profession in the employ of the English East India Company. He had the misfortune to have been stranded from his ship, an English East Indiaman in Buginese territory, where he resided for a while waiting for a ship to take him back to Bengal. He recommended himself favourably to Carteret who took his warning of Dutch duplicity and the Boni threat seriously, particularly when he learnt that he could not only speak the Buginese language but was fluent in Malay, leaving no likelihood of a misunderstanding of their intentions. "Let them come," was his attitude, "800 or 8,000," he told Ray, "that I might have more to kill and to show them what fighting was really like." He also learned how strong was the desire of the King to ally himself with the English in the fight against the Dutch oppressors.

When Carteret became aware of Ray's wish to return to Bengal, he offered to take him to Batavia where he could more easily find a ship, but the young man declined, not wishing to go any deeper into Dutch territory where he would probably end up in prison: anyone coming from Buginese domain would be regarded with deep suspicion. He did not remain long and was soon on his way, a little richer by a quadrant, a few charts and books on navigation.

The breeze which for the past weeks had been blowing fitfully, at last settled in the south-east. It was time to get under weigh and head for Batavia. The distance was little more than 600 miles and with a fair wind, a week should see the *Swallow* not far off. The crew were by now much recovered, not quite all of them, but rest and good food had helped to bring better health to the majority. Fresh meat in the form of four large bullocks was towed out and each hoisted aboard at the yardarm to be butchered later. And now with all hands aboard once again, the sheet anchor was recovered, then one bower anchor. During this last night at Bonthain Bay, the *Swallow* lay at a single bower ready to get under weigh at first light next morning.

At 5.30 a.m. Monday, May 23rd, the anchor was weighed and sail made, and with the guard ship in company, the course was set for Tanjong Petan at the Western Cape of Bonthain Bay. There was a hiccup soon after this when the Purser came to Carteret telling him he believed that the Resident had forgotten to endorse the victualling bills, and on opening the envelopes this was found to be so. Rather than going to all the labour of tacking back to regain the anchorage, the guard vessel was requested to return to Bonthain to get this put right, which they could do with minimum effort being more weatherly than the old *Swallow* with her bluff bows and weed covered bottom. Carteret promised that, in the mean time, he would anchor in shelter between Tanakiki Island and the mainland and wait for her return. The wind was fresh and the *Swallow* bowled along westward with a leadsman in the chains and the pumps going at times, the leaks being as bad as ever, particularly in the bow. By noon she had cleared Bulu Bulu and bore up for Tanakiki Island where at 5.00 p.m. she came to anchor with the small bower to spend the night in shelter. Next morning the guardship returned bearing the documents duly signed and sealed, no time being wasted in sending a boat for them. Once they were in Carteret's hands the two ships each went their own way, the *Swallow* to the west, the guard ship to Macassar, her task finished.

The Monsoon had not yet settled to the east, being variable and uncertain; it brought the rain which soon found its way through the seams in the deck to the seaman's hammocks beneath, and the seas, when they increased, slopped through the gaps in way of the wind and weather timbers above the water line, dried out by the tropical heat.

At 2.30 that afternoon an island hove in sight to the north. As the *Swallow* made her approach it was seen to be one of three, the largest called Laars, according to a chart in Carteret's possession. The course at the time appeared to take her a safe distance off, about four miles, when the water shoaled dangerously, and in no time at all she was in the shallows with great jagged lumps of coral clearly seen close under her keel. It was a near thing! She was on a bowline at the time, so the yards were swiftly boxed round until the sails were aback, and she came off stern first as quickly as she went on without touching. That was the way of it in those waters, "no bottom! no bottom!" came the shout from the chains with a twenty fathom line, then suddenly shoal water before the next call.

As a result of this narrow escape, in order to avoid a repetition, soundings were taken with the deep sea lead at suitable intervals, usually at the change of watch, and again at four bells. This gave fair warning of shoal water ahead, not evident on any chart in Carteret's possession. The deep sea lead weighed 14 lb and was attached to the end of a hundred fathom line. A sounding was a task to be taken with care, and occupied time; the side was manned, each of several seamen with a coil of the lead line in hand; when all was ready the ship was luffed up to take the way off; the lead was cast, each man releasing his coil in succession on the call of the next man ahead of him, until the line became slack at the time when the lead hit the sea bed. In this fashion considerable depths could be plumbed, in the *Swallow's* case a cast of between 40 and 50 fathoms, these being the deepest recorded, with the nature of the sea bed indicated by the arming in the cavity at the base of the lead, mud or clay, sometimes shell. The arming in the cavity consisted of a mixture of white lead and tallow which picked up traces revealing hints of what lay beneath.

The next landfall was Kulkan or Turkey Island. Others were sighted in due course; Masalembo Besar, Bawean or Lombok Island and Kariman Jawa, each one except Bawean surrounded by shallows bestrewn with rocks and reefs. Nothing could jog the old ship beyond three or four knots at best. During the passage to Batavia the seamen were kept busy tending the sails, the wind being so fickle, and also toiling at the pumps. The carpenter, a man of considerable energy, worked on repairing the cutter, and later the longboat, which was found to be much eaten with woodworm and requiring urgent attention. His crew was sadly depleted, one man being laid up with scurvy while the other had lost the use of one hand due to some complaint. However, he went on with the repairs as best as he could with whatever help his one-armed mate could give him.

The unseasonable weather continued unabated: heavy squalls played havoc with the sails particularly the fore and main topsails which had to be sent down for repairs and spare ones bent. The rain which came with the squalls leaked through the deck caulking onto the seamen's hammocks. Sea water was also a problem finding its way through the open seams in the wind and weather strakes into the hold and store rooms. Later, when the opportunity arose, their contents, mainly ropes and sails were brought up on deck to dry out.

Saturday's weather was much the same, while Sunday brought light airs and unsettled weather and with it slow progress. There was a diversion when two waterspouts developed not far off, but fortunately in the end both of them went clear. At noon on Monday, the reef bestrewn island of Kariman Jawa abeam to the south. Carteret gave it a wide berth and by Thursday the *Swallow* was in the approaches to Batavia. The following day, or the day after, would see her safely at anchor. At noon on Friday Carteret shaped the *Swallow* in towards the land with the chains manned and regular soundings called. A sloop at anchor indicated a safe berth, so as it was late in the day, he decided to bring up for the night. The water shoaled gradually as he closed the anchorage, and at 7 o'clock, with 13 fathoms called from the chains, the *Swallow* came to a mooring with the sheet anchor and veered to one cable. Edam Island, Carteret noted, bore north-west two to three miles. The pumps were still going as the anchor went down, the scuppers gushing gallons of clear water overside.

The following morning, when the sea breeze set in, the capstan was manned and the ship brought under easy rail. It was 11 o'clock. The channel through the sand banks was clearly marked with beacons, and by 1 o'clock, using the dome of the Netherlandsche Rock as a marker; the *Swallow* came to anchor in Batavia Roads amongst a throng of ships; eleven large Dutch vessels, one Spanish galleon, a Portuguese snow and numerous small craft including a significant number of Chinese junks. As soon as the anchor was down, Gower was despatched ashore in the cutter to report the ship's arrival to the Governor. It was dark before he returned without having anything significant to report with regard to contact with the Dutch Authorities.

Chapter XIV

Founded in 1619 Batavia, a city and port once known as the 'Jewel of the East', was a little piece of Holland in the Orient. It was a well planned metropolis built on land drained by a criss-cross of rhines and canals. Substantially built residences alongside the waterways reflected the prosperity of the citizens, their wealth generated by the activities of the Dutch East India Company. Here was everything the *Swallow*'s required in the way of ship's stores and shipyard facilities to put her to rights and send her on her way home in good order.

A jewel it may have been in the way of wealth, but it was a most unhealthy city for Europeans. The canals bred mosquitoes which gave malaria to all those bitten by them, and the inhabitants living in this climate, found their health impaired with little resistance to the disease, many of them dying as a result. Those that survived were often left with indifferent health, some of them becoming mere spectres of their former selves.

The following morning, having had no joy from the Dutch Authorities after Gower's visit ashore the previous day, Carteret announced the arrival of His Britannic Majesty's ship *Swallow* in a more positive manner. It was Sunday, the date being June 5th. At sunrise the harbour was wakened by the *Swallow* saluting the fort which guarded the port, with eleven guns. The fort returned the courtesy by firing off a similar number.

Although it was a day when the crew might expect to take it easy being the Sabbath, those who were well enough were exercised at small arms, muskets, pistols, cutlasses and pikes. There were other tasks to be attended to particularly swabbing the decks, cleaning the paintwork and polishing the brass in order to have the *Swallow* looking her best to receive visitors, should they come on board. The carpenter, as busy as ever, went to work on the bottom strakes of the longboat which were found to be badly worm-eaten. Of real importance to ship and crew was the visit of a local small craft bringing with it a consignment of fresh beef. This day also happened to be the birthday of His Majesty King George III, so at 1 p.m. the harbour reverberated with the sound of twenty-one guns fired by the *Swallow* in celebration. After the salute Carteret went ashore in the cutter to wait on the Governor and officially report the ship's arrival.

The reception was not a warm one. His reputation as a prickly, stubborn British Officer had preceded him from Macassar. On being presented to the Governor, Petrus Albertas van der Parra, to give him his full title, he acquainted him with the *Swallow's* condition and urgent requirements, and as he put it, "he desired that he might have the liberty of the port to use their wharfs and store houses, and employ workmen to repair her defects."

The Governor's reply was to inform him coldly that he must first petition the Batavia Council for permission. A letter stating the ship's requirements was needed.

On his return to the *Swallow*, Carteret penned the required letter in which he repeated the verbal request given to the Governor including the wording that he "hoped they would allow him the use of their wharfs and storehouses etc."

By the following day the letter was in the hands of the Council. It did not go down very well with them. On Tuesday three men came on board to discuss the matter, including the Shabander, Paul Godfrey van der Voort, an important gentleman who later became Governor General of Macassar. He knew no English and was accompanied by an English merchant, a certain Mr. Garrison, whose duty it was to interpret. There was a third person in the party, Meheer Thomasson, who appeared to have been brough along as an observer and to take notes of the proceedings.

It was not long before the subject of Nicholas Ray was broached and the matter of a letter sent to Carteret by him. It was understood it contained accusations that Authorities in Macassar had plans to capture the *Swallow* with the help of one of the local Kings! Could they see the letter in order to learn precisely the nature of the threat? If there was any truth in it then the author should be punished.

"What letter?" Carteret maintained that he had never told anyone that there was one. He was adamant about this, so why should they ask him to produce it?

"Was it really so?" they replied "Would he be prepared to take his oath on it, that he had never received one?"

No, he would not! Furthermore, he was surprised that they should make such a request! If the Council had anything to say to him they should put it in writing and he would give them a proper rely. Then, turning to other matters, he desired to know the answer to his letter about the *Swallow*'s repairs.

The Batavia Council, the Shabander informed him, were surprised at his writing that he "hoped" that they might allow him the use of their wharfs and storehouses etc. The word "hope", the Shabander intimated, implied that they might unreasonably refuse his request!

Not so, Carteret assured him. The word "hope" in the English language was well adapted to the subject of his letter, but in his Journal he admits that "begged the favour" might have been more appropriate thus engendering willing co-operation. However, his explanation did not appear to convince his visitors, and on this unsatisfactory note the three men left to make their report to the Council.

There were further visits from the Shabandar, although as yet no favourable reply from the Authorities. To be certain the *Swallow*'s defects were as serious as Carteret made out, a carpenter and his two assistants were sent aboard to verify them. Chief carpenter, Meneer Bouten, was left in no doubt as to her poor condition. Although laying quietly at anchor, he reported that he found twelve and a half inches in the well and that she was leaking to the extent of two inches every hour. What he could see of the hull below the waterline revealing the sheathing to be badly eaten by the toredo worm, and he was in no doubt that some strakes beneath were also affected. On the main deck some planks were very much damaged. In short, they found the whole ship unserviceable inside and out. With regard to the masts and spars, their examination was cursory to say the least, since they reported that they found nothing there to remark on.

This was a surprising statement! The spars and rigging, although weather-worn and bleached were well ordered and seamanlike as befitted a ship of the Royal Navy. But a more careful inspection would have revealed a number of defects, the most serious being rot in the mainyard and bowsprit. Furthermore, they missed seeing six broken chain-plates. Many more defects were found later which were not reported by the carpenters.

There was no apparent hurry in dealing with the *Swallow's* needs by the Batavia Council. Procrastination was very much the order of the day. The Shabander and his assistants made two more visits, one on June 9th and another on June 15th. They brought a complaint from the Council about Carteret's behaviour at Macassar and a protest against his apparent low and mean opinion of them, quite unjustified in their view.

Carteret's reply to the Shabander was to say that if there was any complaint against the ship, it should be put in writing and forwarded to him and he would deal with it accordingly. While he was on the subject he reminded them that he had always adhered to the terms of treaty between their two countries, whereas they on their part had shown particular reluctance to do so.

The days passed with no reply to his letters. In order to speed things up Carteret penned another, stressing more forcefully the *Swallow's* urgent requirements. In the mean time, finding the need to spend a day or two ashore to deal with the ship's business, he put up for a night at a hotel where visitors of some importance who were not Dutch citizens, were required to lodge. During his time ashore Carteret made use of a coach which most people did on account of the heat. When meeting on the road with the Governor or members of the Batavia Council certain formalities had to be observed and the Landlord of the hostel, on the instructions of the Shabandar, informed Carteret of them.

He could not fail to recognise the Governor's coach. It was escorted by armed troopers and preceded by two footmen with canes whose duty it was to clear the way, beating people cruelly if they did not observe proper homage. Should such a meeting occur, Carteret, like others, whether gentleman, merchant, priest or peasant must, without exception, draw into the side of the road, alight and bow most humbly to his Excellency. Any disinclination to conform to this custom would be sure to affect relations with the Governor and Council, and in retaliation the coachman would be sought out and severely chastised. Similarly, the members of the Batavia Council expected to receive homage with the difference that the person meeting them need only stop his coach and stand up in it to make his bow.

Carteret was not slow in perceiving that this folly could not possibly apply to him, a Captain of the British Navy. His Majesty King George did not expect even the lowest of his subjects to submit to such servile grovelling. He made this quite clear, telling the Landlord to inform the Shabandar that he declined to take part in such folly. "I should not suffer my carriage to stop for any person whatsoever," he told him adamantly, making it quite clear that if anyone seriously approached him to make him conform, he was prepared to defend himself. He said this pointing to the loaded pistols on the table. At this, the Landlord wasted no time in informing the Shabandar, who made the Governor aware of his intentions. Three hours later the Landlord returned with the message that he might do as he pleased.

At some time during the week, the carpenter's report of the *Swallow*'s condition eventually reached the desk of the man in charge of nautical affairs in Batavia, Vice-Admiral Nicholaas Houtingh. He was the Commander of the Dutch East India Company's Navy in the Far East, and in this gentleman, Carteret had at last found a friend, someone who understood the real needs of an old vessel on a long voyage, many thousand miles away from her home port. When the Council at last decided to allow the *Swallow* to use the facilities of the port, this gentleman gave instructions for repairs to be put in hand with very little further delay.

On June 18th, everything was at last in hand. The *Swallow*, according to the Vice-Admiral's orders, was to proceed to a neighbouring island where all the facilities for careening existed. Once there, a ship was to be made available to take on board her stores. On Wednesday, June 22nd, she left her moorings, and with a Dutch pilot on board, was taken to the island of Onrust where she came to anchor. The Dutch East India ship *Bladort* was brought alongside to receive her stores and when they were unloaded, it was the turn of the ballast to be discharged. After this she was warped alongside a wharf at Kuiper or Cooper's Island as Carteret called it, where with her upper yards and soars on deck and topmasts housed, she was all set for the task of heaving down.

While these preparations were going on the *Dudley*, an English ship recently in from Bengal, came to anchor nearby. She was in desperate need of heaving down with her sheathing and hull so badly worm-eaten she was in worse danger of foundering than the *Swallow*. Her Captain came to see Carteret, begging him that he might precede him to the careening berth to which he agreed, providing Vice-Admiral Houtingh gave permission.

Although Carteret had little to say in favour of the Governor and Council, and Dutch officialdom in general, he had nothing but praise for the Vice-Admiral. The difference in attitude between them was most apparent, the former regarding the *Swallow* and her crew as little more than adventurers, while the Vice-Admiral understood the loneliness and frustration a Captain could meet in a foreign port. As a young man he had learnt his seamanship in English men-of-war and consequently had a fine command of the English language. The cordial relationship between the two men continued all through the time the *Swallow* was at the careenage with Carteret often in the Vice-Admiral's company, having a general invitation to his table. He saw no reason against the *Dudley* having precedence over the *Swallow* in a case of such dire need, and so it was arranged. Not surprisingly, this was another black mark against Carteret as far as the Governor and Council were concerned: one day this English Captain was all impatience to have the best attention for his decrepit little ship in order to resume his voyage as soon as possible, and here he was making no bones about allowing another ship to have precedence at the careenage.

In spite of the poor relationship with the Governor and Council, Carteret was honoured with an invitation to a banquet to be held on Sunday, August 7th. This particular day was the anniversary of the birth of the Princess of Orange Nassau, whose marriage to the Prince of Nassau had recently taken place. The

Prince himself was an important personage with the titles of Captain and Admiral of the Dutch Republic, and Superior Governor General of the Netherlands East India Company. Neither of these noble persons were to be present, but that did not diminish the importance of the banquet. Yet here again the question of precedence came to mind, and to make quite sure that he would not find himself seated below the wrong people, he paid a visit to the Governor to learn what to expect.

He found him at his Residency in the city, taking his exercise in the garden. His reception was a chilly one; no particular welcome, no invitation to step into the house, in fact no offer of hospitality at all, perhaps not surprising under the circumstances. He had taken the precaution of having an English merchant to accompany him as an interpreter to make sure there was no misunderstanding, and having acquainted the Governor of the reason for the visit, he was very soon informed that he must expect to sit below the members of the Council who would not have it any other way.

At this Carteret made it quite clear that he was unwilling to accept this discourtesy. "I told him," he wrote in his Journal, "that on no account could I submit to such treatment and I should consider myself unworthy of the commission I had the honour to bear in His Majesty's Service if I did." This lack of courtesy was bad enough, but he was further upset when he learnt that he was expected to sit among the Captains of the Merchant ships who had also been invited, namely Captain Thomson of the *Calcutta* and Captain Roddham of the *Harcourt*, both without doubt worthy men and fine seamen, but being 'in trade' as they were, he was reluctant to sit with them. This would have brought wry smiles from the two Captains and remarks about pompous Royal Navy Officers. Masters of Merchant ships held the title of Captain only by courtesy and were some way down the social scale in Carteret's opinion. But to be fair to him, although his expectations might appear unreasonable, he had no wish to cause any dissension which might affect their trading, as might have been the case had he felt it behoved him to walk out of the banquet.

The *Dudley*'s repairs kept her at the careenage for the best part of a month, and it was not until July 24th was the *Swallow* able to be warped into the berth. With tackles rigged from her mastheads to the shore she was, in due course, hove down on her beam ends.

When the hull was fully exposed, it revealed the wooden sheathing to be completely worm-eaten. There was worse to come! The removal of the sheathing exposed a number of strakes in the hull itself, which the sheathing was supposed to protect, to be also badly attacked by the worm. The Dutch carpenters, seeing this, wanted to remove much of the bottom and replace it, something Carteret wished to avoid at all cost, fearing that if they probed too deeply, perhaps revealing extensive rot in the timbers, the ship might be condemned as unseaworthy; the crew dispersed or thrown on the beach, and the whole voyage ending in failure. As it was, an amazing number of defects came to light: in addition to the bowsprit and mainyard, a further seven chainplates required to be replaced. Several beam knees were found to be loose, also the butt ends of a number of strakes, particularly at the stem, where there were gaps large enough for a man to insert his hand. And this was only on one side. When the repairs were complete with the sheathing in place again, the ship had to be righted, turned around and hove down again, for the other side to be dealt with. This was found to be in much the same state of decay requiring similar significant attention.

During this period all hands had to live and sleep ashore, it being impossible to stay on board a ship hove down. As far as the crew were concerned, the repairs could not be completed too quickly. Many of them were now so ill that a hospital under canvas had to be set up ashore to receive them. However, it did not prevent a death toll which reached altogether a total of twenty-one of the crew. All this was in spite of the attention of

Surgeon Watson and his assistant, and the best meat and vegetables which Batavia could supply. Among those so ill was young Kerton, who kept such a faithful log of the voyage. Fortunately, he recovered, although not in time to sail with the ship.

By mid-September all the repairs were completed and everything in train for the *Swallow* to sail for home. It was early in the season as Admiral Houtingh pointed out: most ships bound for Europe delayed sailing until December, when wind and weather were more favourable with less likelihood of storms off the Cape of Good Hope. On his part, Carteret was anxious to be gone and prepared to take the weather as it came. It only remained to find enough seamen to bring the numbers to a full complement. There were still many sick men on board and more would die if the ship was delayed much longer.

By good fortune there was no problem in finding crew. When the news spread around that the *Swallow* was about to sail, 21 seamen, mostly English, presented themselves, deserters from Dutch or other ships who had been caught by the press gang in home waters and now desperate to join a ship bound for England. As the time to leave drew near, Carteret fell ill with a troublesome fever and was unable to wait on the Governor, a formality which was expected of him before putting to sea. In his place he sent Gower to do the honours, instructing him, as an act of courtesy, to inquire if there were any despatches the Governor might wish to be taken to Europe. Although Gower did as requested the offer was not taken up.

Chapter XV

Sailing day for the *Swallow* came at last. On September 15th, 1768, a Thursday, she took her departure from the Island of Onrust making for the Straits of Sunda. She was in as good order with regard to hull, masts and rigging as ever the Dutch shipwrights could make her; and in respect of provisions, well stocked up for the long voyage across the Indian Ocean to Cape Town. The exception was wood and water which Carteret intended to make good in some convenient bay in the Sunda Strait before finally leaving the coast.

Passing Amsterdam Island to starboard, by midday the *Swallow* was clear of Batavia Bay and heading for St Nicholas Point at the entrance to the Sunda Strait. Carteret had no intention of navigating the Strait during the hours of darkness, so at 6 p.m., the *Swallow* was brought to anchor with the small bower. Sickness was still claiming men's lives with Seaman Phillip York dying that night. The crew continued to suffer the effects of the Batavia climate with more and more men dying as the days passed.

Friday morning came with light airs and the *Swallow* drifting into the Strait with the boats out ready to tow her clear of any shoals encountered. Although these were waters where the Dutch held sway, Carteret fixed the ship's noon position by bearings of islands with English names: Copper, Button and

Thwartway written in his log. When approaching Thwartway Island, which lay in the middle of the Strait, the *Swallow* was seen to be caught by the current and relentlessly set in towards an area of disturbed water, and in spite of every effort to make her bear off, nothing all hands could do persuaded her to comply. Over she went, reef, rock, sandbank or whatever, not even the cutter and longboat towing her, their crews pulling with all their might, achieved anything and in the end she ploughed her own course into the turmoil regardless. A sounding at the time, gave a good four fathoms under her keel as it happened, and soon very after, she was through it into deeper water again, when all hands could heave a sigh of relief. At 6 p.m., she was brought to anchor off Old Anjer for the night.

September 20th, a Tuesday, came in with unsettled squally weather. During the first dog watch that evening the *Swallow* was beset by a particularly heavy rain squall accompanied by terrible claps of thunder and blinding flashes of lightning. The signs were there of more to come and the sails were clewed up, as the *Swallow* lay to the blast under bare poles. Fortunately the squall, severe though it was, soon passed and the visibility improved until sunset when all sight of land was lost in the darkness. Meanwhile the course was altered towards the shore looking for shallower water, and when a cast of the lead showed thirty fathoms, the *Swallow* was brought to anchor for the night.

Sunrise on Wednesday revealed the peak of Princes Island to the west. By 2.30 that afternoon the *Swallow* was able to stand in for the watering place which lay on the south-eastern side. At 4 o'clock she was brought to a mooring with the best bower forward and the stream anchor aft. This was an uneasy berth on a lee shore with troublesome surf breaking on the beach: plenty of wood available, but when a search was made for water the only source was found to be almost dry, in fact quite insufficient to fill all the casks needed to see the ship to the Cape. The season had been an unusually poor one, as they learnt from the few inhabitants they managed to make contact with. Those that they did were fishermen and friendly enough, only were particularly reluctant to communicate with English ships, the penalty being death or slavery if the Dutch found out. This lack of concourse was a disappointment, since trading for fish or fowl always brought a welcome change from the daily ration of salt beef or pork, although it is doubtful if the lower deck shared much in it: a large number of chickens would be needed to satisfy a hungry crew of the *Swallow*'s complement. Turtle was an alternative, and the fishermen agreed to trade, but only after sunset when a meeting could take place undetected in the dark.

The water situation was a particular disappointment and another watering place had to be found directly. Herbert's 'New Dictionary for the Indies' held information about another suitable one across the Strait in the narrow channel between Mew Island and the Java shore: it lay dead to windward a distance of six miles with no possibility of getting the *Swallow* there at present, not even using sweeps or the boats to tow her over. However, the time was not wasted, and on Thursday a working party was put ashore to cut and collect wood, and to save time should the wind become more favourable, the stream anchor was won.

Ferrying the few casks of water obtained through the surf to the ship was no problem, but the wood was a different proposition. Plans were put in hand to haul it out on rafts to the calmer water by means of a warp to the boats which lay to a grapnel beyond the breakers. It was then towed out to the *Swallow*; load after load of it, altogether a slow, tedious task. And now a quantity of ballast was called for in order to adjust her draft to the correct sailing trim, In this respect gravel was available on shore, any amount of it, so quantities of this were carried out through the surf to the boats beyond in buckets balanced on the seamen's heads. In due course this was done, the wood and gravel occupying three days of intensive labour.

By Monday morning the wind had moderated sufficiently to make sail and take the *Swallow* over to Mew Island. Although only a short distance across the Strait, with the wind persistently in the south-east, it proved to be a tedious beat during which the first board brought her perilously close to the rocks off Princes Island before she reached more open water. She was close enough to disaster for Carteret to make a note of it in the log, and it was touch and go before, by good fortune, she won clear. Seven hours later, after several tedious boards, she came at last to anchor with the best bower in fourteen fathoms in a sheltered bay close by Mew Island. It had taken eight and a half hours to achieve those six miles to windward, a worthwhile effort altogether as the water on the Java side of the little strait was not only easily accessible but was of excellent quality.

It cascaded down from the rocks straight into the sea, making it possible to fill the casks without taking them from the boats. So that the casks could be filled without taking them from the boats. There was a small reef which formed a basin where the boats could lay in safety completely protected from the swell. Altogether it was a fine place to stock up, plenty of wood available and the water was so good that Carteret ordered all the casks filled at Batavia and Princes Island to be started, except the bottom tier, and refilled with it, soon the boats were plying back and forth filling the casks with comparative ease, and while this was being done, a working party was put ashore to cut wood for the galley. When watering was completed it amounted to 37 tons (over 9,000 gallons).

The morning of Thursday, September 25th, occupied the *Swallow*'s crew taking on board the last boatloads of wood. Preparations were now put in hand for sailing. At 7 o'clock next morning the windlass was manned, the anchor weighed and with a fresh breeze from the SSE, the *Swallow's* course was shaped out of the Strait between Princes Island and Java Head. These were waters which in later years were familiar to seaman of the 'Tea-Clippers', many features of the coast on the charts bearing English names, for example, Carpenter Rocks lay on the *Swallow*'s starboard hand as she cleared the Strait, and Friar Rocks to port, Welcome Bay, Thwartway and Button Islands come to mind while nearby headlines came under the names

Second Point, Third Point and Fourth Point.

Soon after the *Swallow* cleared Java Head, the breeze backed south-easterly which allowed the course to be set south-west for the Cape of Good Hope, five thousand miles away. The ill-health which so long affected the crew in the West Indies continued unabated with seven men dying on passage before the coast of South Africa was raised. Many more seamen were ill and off duty so that each watch could only muster seventeen men able to hand, reef and steer. Carteret himself was in a bad way with sickness and fever but with great determination managed to keep command in spite of it all. By November 23rd the *Swallow* was nearing the African Coast and being in sounding was feeling the effect of the Agulhus Current which, with the prevailing SW wind set up a particularly steep sea with the crests breaking on board. Five days later, November 28th, Cape Town was in sight and the *Swallow*, having saluted the fort with eleven guns, came to anchor in the Table Bay, forty days out from the Straits of Sunda.

It was a relief to Carteret to find the Dutch Authorities vastly more reasonable and friendly in every respect from their compatriots in their East Indies possessions, particularly those in Batavia. "I could scarcely believe the people of this place were of the same nation," he wrote in his Journal, "where nothing else reigns but Pride, Insolence, Jealousy, Suspicion and Mistrust. The temperate climate might have something to do with their good nature, also the pleasant countryside." He had a special mention for Meneer Ryk Tulbagh, the Governor of Cape Colony who was not only a just and enlightened man but a patron of the sciences. He also happened to be a relative by marriage of Sergius Swellengrabel, the gentleman who treated Carteret so kindly at Bonthaine. Other officials who came in for commendation were Jan Willem Cloppenburg and Joachim Van Pluttenberg, who dealt with the finances of the Colony. On the social side, he was introduced to the first secretary of the Dutch east India Company, a Meneer Barrawkee who found time to provide him with his report on the giraffe, an animal practically unknown in Europe and of such interest to Carteret that he penned a letter with its description and measurements together with a drawing to his friend Matthew Maty, the Secretary of the Royal Society.

During the weeks at anchor no ships came in from the East Indies but the *Sneok*, a Dutch vessel recently in from Holland, came to a mooring nearby. Her Captain, one Meneer Stavorinus by name, desired to know all he could about the *Swallow's* voyage which in fact, was very little, since if Carteret had given an account of it to his Dutch friends, they kept much of it to themselves: the only information he managed to glean concerned the visit to Juan Fernandez. This merited a mention in Barrawkee's book, 'Voyages', published in 1798. Although the *Swallow* and the *Snoek* remained together in the bay for three weeks, the two captains never met.

The *Swallow's* visit to Cape Town did much to bring her crew to good health again, but to achieve this required a longer stay than intended. A whole month passed before all was sufficiently in hand to leave, and in the end Christmas went by, then New Year, and as time went on another week slipped by while waiting for a fair wind. This eventually came away on January 6th when she was at last able to make sail. The next port of call was St. Helena.

The 1,700 miles to St. Helena occupied fourteen days of leisurely sailing. On January 20th at 1 o'clock in the afternoon, the *Swallow* came to anchor off the little port of Jamestown after a passage which Carteret declared had been a pleasant one blessed with a fair wind all the way, and some days sailing exceeding 120 miles. This volcanic island, a mere speck in the ocean, ten and a half miles long by six and a half miles wide, was a useful place to break the long haul up the South Atlantic and stock up with provisions and water, and also to catch up on the latest news from Europe, particularly as to which countries might be at war with Great Britain at that time this island was appropriated by the Honourable East India Company in the previous century, later becoming a British possession, famous as Napoleon's place of exile from which he was least likely to escape.

The news at St Helena was good: peace reigned in Europe although Russia and Turkey were soon to be at odds and the American Colonies were restless, wanting their independence and freedom from the rule of George III. Four days later the *Swallow* was on her way again. The next port of call was the little island of Ascension[25]. This was sighted to the westward at midnight on January 30th, the visibility being so clear at the time. She was brought to until daylight when the land was close, looking for Cross Hill Bay, where Carteret believed he would find shelter. Being unsure where this was, he set the course up the eastern side close inshore with the cutter ahead leading the way, until a likely bay, which fitted the description of the one he was looking for, came into view. The cross, erected by a visiting ship many years before, was there on the hill clearly seen from seaward, with the promise of a good mooring in the bay within. Certainly, it was not one to be passed by without investigating.

Soon after entering the bay, Carteret brought the *Swallow* to anchor close by a sandy beach with good access to the shore. Few ships had reason to call here except those wishing to obtain fresh food in the form of turtles of which there were plenty and easily captured from the beach near the anchorage. At some time in the past, the crew of a visiting ship had rigged a rope ladder for easy access to the shore where messages in bottles were left in a conspicuous place. The island itself, uninhabited at the time of the *Swallow's* visit, had little to offer except the turtles and water, being little more than a volcanic mass thrown up from the sea-bed, rather barren in the lower parts. In contrast,

---

[25] Ascension Island became a British possession in 1815 as a precautionary measure against any attempt to rescue Napoleon from St Helena. The military post created there became known as Georgetown.

the highest elevation called Green Mountain, 2,820 feet above sea-level, was frequently covered in cloud and appeared to contain verdant pastureland.

A working party was sent ashore that evening to capture turtles and turn them on their backs to be collected later next morning. They brought back altogether eighteen large specimens weighing from four to six hundredweight, each sufficient for all hands to have fresh meat for dinner that day. Their numbers were indeed prolific and many more could have been taken but there was insufficient space on deck to stow them. With fresh water and turtles on board there was nothing further to delay the *Swallow*; that evening Tuesday, February 1st, she set sail for the last leg of the voyage home.

Chapter XVI

In the light winds of equatorial waters, the *Swallow's* progress was predictably slow. Nineteen days after leaving Ascension Island, she had only reached latitude 13° N, a distance of 1,260 miles with a daily average of 63. Some days she achieved more, others she lay becalmed and sweltering in the tropical heat. On Tuesday, February 20th, a vessel hove in sight to leeward coming up close hauled apparently intending to make contact. It was a long chase lasting all that day and through the following night. Not until noon next day was she close enough to communicate. She proved to be the French ship *La Boudeuse* commanded by Compte Louis de Bougainville, which like the *Swallow* was homeward bound after her round the world voyage.

There was nothing unusual in a stranger hailing another, surely a matter of courtesy between two ships meeting in the open sea. However there was some surprise aboard the *Swallow* when Carteret's name was mentioned and his health inquired after. There was more to come. The *Dolphin* had arrived home they were informed and it was thought in England that the *Swallow* had been wrecked. Two ships were to be sent to look for her. The information, so Bouganville said, had come from a French India Company's ship returning from the Far East. Was there anything the *Swallow* required, and if so *La Boudeuse* could supply him, refreshment particularly was mentioned, or despatches and letters for home or Europe perhaps.

Carteret thanked him for his obliging offers at the same time wondering how the Frenchman could suppose there was need of anything the *Swallow* should require having visited the same places as *La Boudeuse*. With regard to letters he suggested that, if Bougainville thought it proper, he might send a boat over to take those he had received from some French gentleman at the Cape which could then go directly to France rather than going via England. When the two ships were hove to the Frenchman sent a cutter over. This was something not to be missed on the part of Bougainville who was pleased to take the opportunity it offered of learning about the *Swallow*'s discoveries during the Pacific crossing. He did not accompany the cutter himself, sending someone to deputise for him.

On his part Carteret had no intention of divulging anything. He was unsure what to make of the young man who came with the cutter, not a ship's officer by his appearance, a passenger perhaps, or supercargo, quite unofficerlike in dress and manner. Nonetheless, he received him in the Grand Cabin with polite reserve, and after the customary compliments, the young man repeated Bougainville's offer of refreshments if he should require any.

This offer was politely declined and after these formalities, Carteret inquired of the young man what had brought *La Boudeuse* homeward so much earlier in the season for ships involved in the Eastern trade. His answer was evasive and vague: some of the cargo had been left at the Isle de France for people's needs or those of other ships calling there. The real purpose of the early return was due to some dispute between the Governor and local inhabitants, and *La Bouduese* was charged with important dispatches on this account. After some further conversation, it became clear that the answers Carteret received were evasive and lacking in interest. The young man on his part was in no hurry to end the conversation and continued to ask pertinent questions revealing considerable knowledge of the

Swallow's adventures touching on the problems encountered with Indians and the unfortunate loss of an officer.

Then there were questions, among others, concerning the *Swallow*'s suitability for the task she had been set which Carteret, finding himself irritated by such remarks, was quite unwilling to discuss. After a while he rose to his feet indicating that, as if as he was concerned, the interview was at an end. Going to his cabin to find a small gift to send Bougainville for his obliging civilities, he found the young man following him, both confused and upset while at the same time trying to say something to recover himself and continue the discussion. Carteret however, would have none of it, and after saying that he wished to make sail immediately, the young man left.

The abrupt departure and demeanour of the Frenchman did not pass unnoticed and when Carteret came on deck to make sail, Lieutenant Gower was moved to say that he hoped the visit had not been too much of an imposition. He had already learnt something of *La Boudeuses*' voyage from one of the *Swallow*'s seamen who hailed from Quebec; being fluent in French he understood from one of the crew of the cutter a few details, particularly about difficulties encountered in the Straits of Magellan which had lengthened their voyage by several months. And now, the usual courtesies having been exchanged, the two vessels parted. *La Boudeuse*, despite being foul below her water-line after her long Pacific voyage, showed the *Swallow* a clean pair of heels, although she, in her turn set every stitch of canvas possible. "They went by us as if we were at anchor," wrote Carteret in his Journal.

Early in March, the *Swallow* was nearing the Azores. On the 7th, Monday, she was in sight of land when the course was set to pass between the islands of San Miguel and Teneira. Not long after this she had a taste of the turbulent waters of the North Atlantic: on Friday the wind came out of the west blowing hard and increasing in strength all the time until it reached a full gale, bringing up a mighty sea. The warnings were there, so the

Swallow was made as snug as possible in good time by powering the main yard, followed by the mizen topmast and yard being struck. After this she ran comfortably enough until somewhere around 10 o'clock in the evening watch, the roping at the foot of the foresail parted, causing it to split and blow to tatters before the yard could be got down to save it. With no sail she was unable to hold her course and was brought to the wind and sea to be a-try all night under mizen storm staysail. At daylight on Saturday, a new foresail was roused out from the sail room, and having been bent, the yard was hoisted again. This done the ship resumed her course, scudding before the storm. As time went on the wind veered north-westerly until she could no longer run with safety and at 6 o'clock that evening she had to be hove to once more.

And so she remained, Saturday night and all Sunday while the storm raged, and not before daylight on Monday did it moderate sufficiently for the weary crew to put her on course again. According to Carteret's reckoning, the *Swallow* should by now be nearing the English Channel; a cast of the deep-sea lead might confirm this one way or another. When done the result gave no bottom at 150 fathoms, the estimated longitude being too optimistic. Twenty-four hours later another cast was more promising, the depth together with a latitude by meridian altitude indicating that the *Swallow* would shortly be in the 'chops of the Channel. On Wednesday, March 19th, the coast of England could be clearly seen to larboard, and, to the great joy of all hands, Start Point was passed the same day. Next in sight were the Needles, then the Isle of Wight, the fair wind favouring the *Swallow* all the way until the anchor went down for the last time off Spithead. It was Thursday, March 20th, the voyage having lasted two years and seven months.

Carteret wasted no time in sending a letter to the Admiralty Secretary requesting him to inform heir Lordships of the *Swallow's* arrival at Spithead. Included in the letter was a concise account of the voyage with its discoveries, modest though they were. Nonetheless, his achievements might have been more highly regarded had it not been for his nature to grumble rather than make the most of circumstances which he could not improve. Complaints about the *Swallow*'s shortcomings appear in his letter to the Admiralty no less than four times no less.

He also complained of not having enough officers to cover all duties required of a ship engaged on a long voyage of exploration. Perhaps for this reason the reply from the Admiralty Secretary gave no hint of welcome, merely instructing him to attend their Lordships as soon as convenient bringing with him the Abstracts of the voyage together with his journal and logbook. Their lordships also required all charts, plans and drawings made by him during the course of the voyage. Furthermore the Secretary particularly requested that he would collect all log books and journals kept by the *Swallow*'s officers and petty officers: these were to be sealed up and brought the Admiralty Office for their Lordship's inspection.

What their Lordships thought about these documents is not apparent. They brought neither Carteret nor members of his crew any immediate rewards an in themselves had little impact in the realms of navigation: even Pitcairn, the best known of his discoveries brings Hetcher Christian and the Bounty mutinies to mind before Carteret and the *Swallow*. The discovery of St. George's Channel however was a considerable boon to navigators opening up a clear way from the Solomon Sea into the island studded waters of the Western Pacific. He also brought to the notice of mariners the advantages of the Macassar Strait, all of which helped to encourage trade in those waters. Unlike Wallis, and in spite of their early separation, Carteret adhered to the commands of their Lordships in pursuing a course across the Pacific in search of the Great Southern Continent. In the end, it was the condition of the *Swallow* which forced him to abandon the search and seek a place of refuge for repairs to the ship and recovery of the crew from the ravages of scurvy. One wonders if their Lordships appreciated this.

The Admiralty, wishing to make the most of recent discoveries in the Pacific, employed a man of letters to edit the journals of contemporary explorers. Mr John Hawkesworth was chosen for this and in 1773 the 'Voyages' was published. It came out in three volumes taken from the journals of Byron, Wallis, Carteret and Cook, and in due course was translated into other languages. When Carteret cam to read it he found that with regard to the *Swallow's* circumnavigation, the arduous nature of the Pacific crossing had not been satisfactorily told; furthermore important events had been toned down or even disregarded. Hawkesworth's 'Voyages' has not survived, but in view of his misgivings about it Carteret wrote his own account. His 'Journal' stands as an honest and accurate portrayal of an eighteenth century voyage of discovery.

Having no immediate commission from the Admiralty, Carteret returned to Trinity Manor, his home on the Isle of Jersey, to await their Lordship's pleasure. Not being one to enjoy a life of idleness he entered into local politics where he soon made his presence felt. In time, the rumblings of war with Spain brought him to London in the hope of a commission. Early in 1771 he was appointed Captain of the frigate *Flamborough* that had twenty guns. In the end, this came to nothing, and indeed may have been a ploy by the Admiralty to keep him quiet for a while as the *Flamborough* was in bad way requiring expensive repairs amounting to more than her original cost of building. However, he derived some benefit from this having in the mean time been promoted, returning home with the rank of captain.

March 1772 brought him back to London for his wedding to Miss Marie Rachel, a French lady. In due course, he returned to Jersey with her to set up home at Trinity Manor. If the Lords of the Admiralty considered that he might now settle down to the life of a gentleman of ample means and leisure they were disappointed. He continued to press for a ship had high hopes for one when England went to war with the American Colonists in

1775; but time went on with no ship, not even when France joined the conflict the following year.

In contrast to this cavalier treatment, Gower, after a period of unemployment enjoyed a steady rise in his profession having five commissions between 1769 and 1790. His first after leaving the *Swallow* was to the *Swift*, her sister-ship, bound for the Falklands. His appointment was as a Lieutenant, with the promise of promotion to captain in due course. Unfortunately for him she was wrecked at Port Desire near the entrance to the Straits of Magellan, and thus delayed his promotion indefinitely.

1775 found him first Lieutenant of the Frigate *Levant* and in 1779, Lieutenant of the Frigate *Sandwich*. After distinguished service in the West Indies in 1781 he was rewarded with promotion to Captain of the Frigate *Medea* for service in the Far East, followed by three on the Newfoundland Station 1786 to 1789. His next command was the transport Lion, the ship which was chosen to take Lord Macartney and his embassy to China, for which he was rewarded with a Knighthood. This mission appeared to be the end of his sea service. However, his promotion continued becoming rear-admiral in 1799 and an admiral ten years later.

The year 1779 at last brought a change in Carteret's fortunes when he was given command of the Frigate *Endymion*. His first task was to patrol the Channel. She put to sea on October 31st and was soon in trouble. She was caught in a gale, causing enough damage to send her back to port for repairs. This misfortune kept her there throughout the winter. Spring 1780 found her at sea again on patrol on the lookout for ships intending to make French ports with much needed supplies. On occasions the wrong ships were detained resulting in claims made against the *Endymion* and Carteret having to foot the bill. The Admiralty were notoriously unwilling to pay for such errors as in the case of a Danish ship the *De Mathie*. This vessel claimed to be wrongfully detained requiring £870 cost and damage against the Endymion altogether a tidy sum for Carteret to find.

On June 10th, the *Endymion* sailed for Senegal having on board a contigent of soldiers with orders to attack the French settlement there. The Commanding Officer at Goree in change of affairs out there was uncooperative so eventually the plan was abandoned. The *Endymion* then sailed for the West Indies. She was in Barbados on September 19th. The following month when on passage to Martinique she had the misfortune to be overtaken by a hurricane which devastated the Leeward Islands and brought the *Endymion* to the brink of foundering. She was so long overdue that both in England and the Leeward Islands she was thought to be lost, even to the extent of condolences being sent to Lady Carteret on the death of her husband. Against all odds, she arrived safely at Port Royal on March 30th 1781 with her masts in a state of disarray. She had suffered a bad time during which Carteret was nearly killed receiving a blow to his head when he fell at the height of a storm. This laid him up for a while. On the credit side, after the storm two French prizes were taken on the return to port.

While at Port Royal the decision was made to send the *Endymion* home under jury rig for dockyard repairs. Soon she was on her way at the same time making herself useful shepherding a convoy. Here again while doing this she had the good fortune to capture two American prizes.

This unexpected return so early in the commission should have been a happy event, but to Carteret's bitter disappointment he was paid off on arrival at Portsmouth for no apparent reason, and the command of the Endymion given to another captain. Understandably this unexpected dismissal appeared to him as a deliberate slight by the Admiralty. It pointed to a lack of patience with him as a result of his letters of complaint, too frequent for their Lordships to stomach. Even Lord Sandwich, who had given him patronage for so long, appeared to have withdrawn his favour.

At some period in the year 1780 he had found time to move from Jersey to set up home where he would be at the centre of naval affairs rather than in the isolation of the Channel Islands. He still had expectations of another sea-going command, but as time went on without this happening he informed the Admiralty that he would welcome home duty, a lieutenancy at Greenwich Hospital or the old *Royal William*, a guard ship anchored in the Thames. The Admiralty, in their wisdom, gave him no consideration for either of these posts.

As the years went by his family steadily increased with Rachel bearing him five children, Sylvester, Philip, Caroline, Elizabeth and one other, the youngest, who did not survive, By 1883 his health had become indifferent, no doubt brought on early due to the harsh conditions of life at sea. In a letter to Gower he described his ailments as 'rheumatic complaints'. However, by 1784 he had recovered sufficiently to inform the Admiralty that he was ready for service again. In spite of his frequent requests he received no further appointments or any recognition of his achievements from their Lordships. He appears to have suffered a stroke in 1792, and soon after this he was retired with the rank of Rear Admiral. He survived another four years, going to his final resting place in 1796 at an age of 58 years.

Although not so well known amongst those navigators who explored and charted the oceans, Philip Carteret deserves to be remembered for his role in opening up the Pacific. He was a fine seaman; conscientious in his duties, having at all times particular consideration for his crew who returned his care for them with unstinting loyalty. The *Swallow* was not the best of ships for the task and she required great skill and determination to take her safely round the world and home again, an achievement which was altogether a credit to both Carteret and her crew.

Illustrations

Philip Carteret

Samuel Wallis

Model of the *Swallow*

(Cover Illustration) The *Swallow* by H.G. Mowat

(Pages 204 and 205) Cross-sections of the *Swallow*

(Page 206) The *Swallow's* Pacific Crossing compared with Anson, Byron, Wallis & Cook

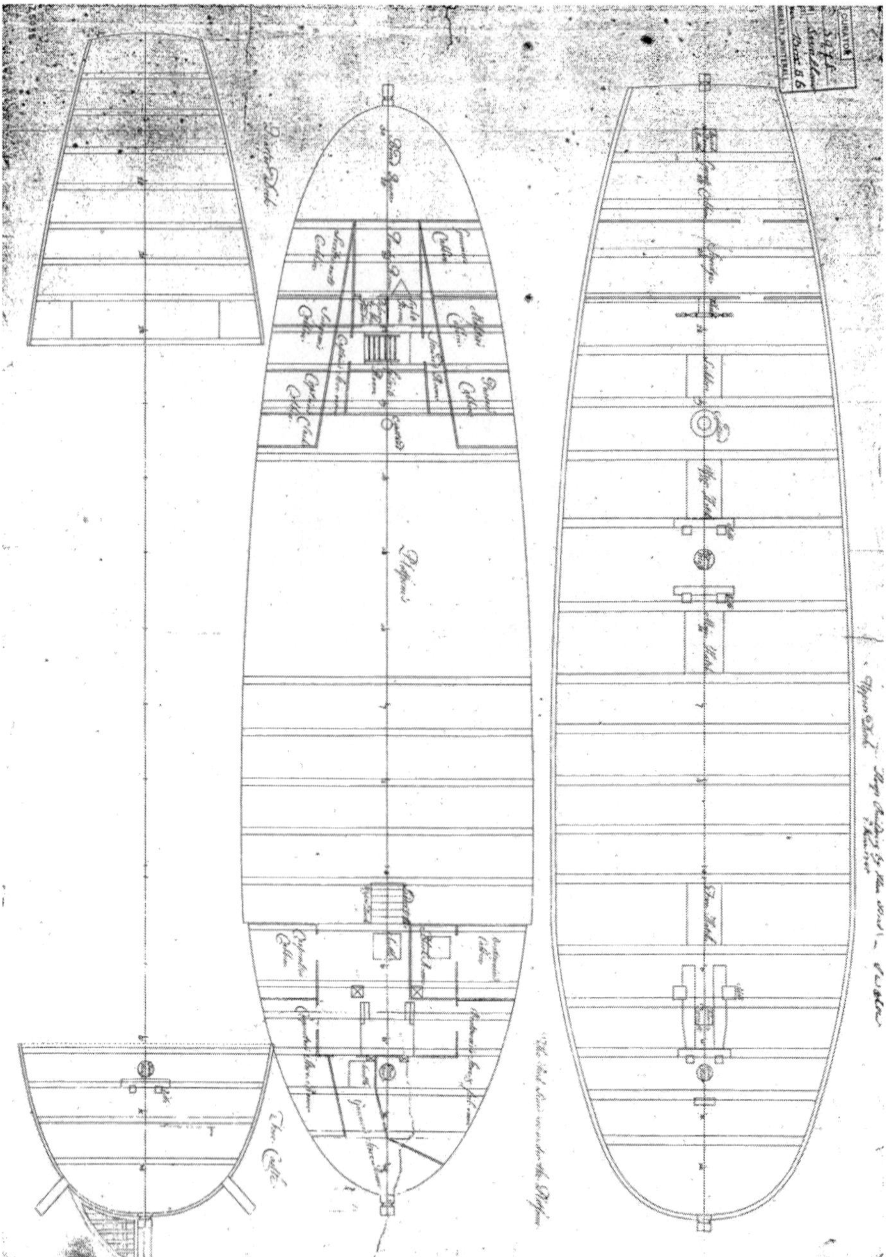

205

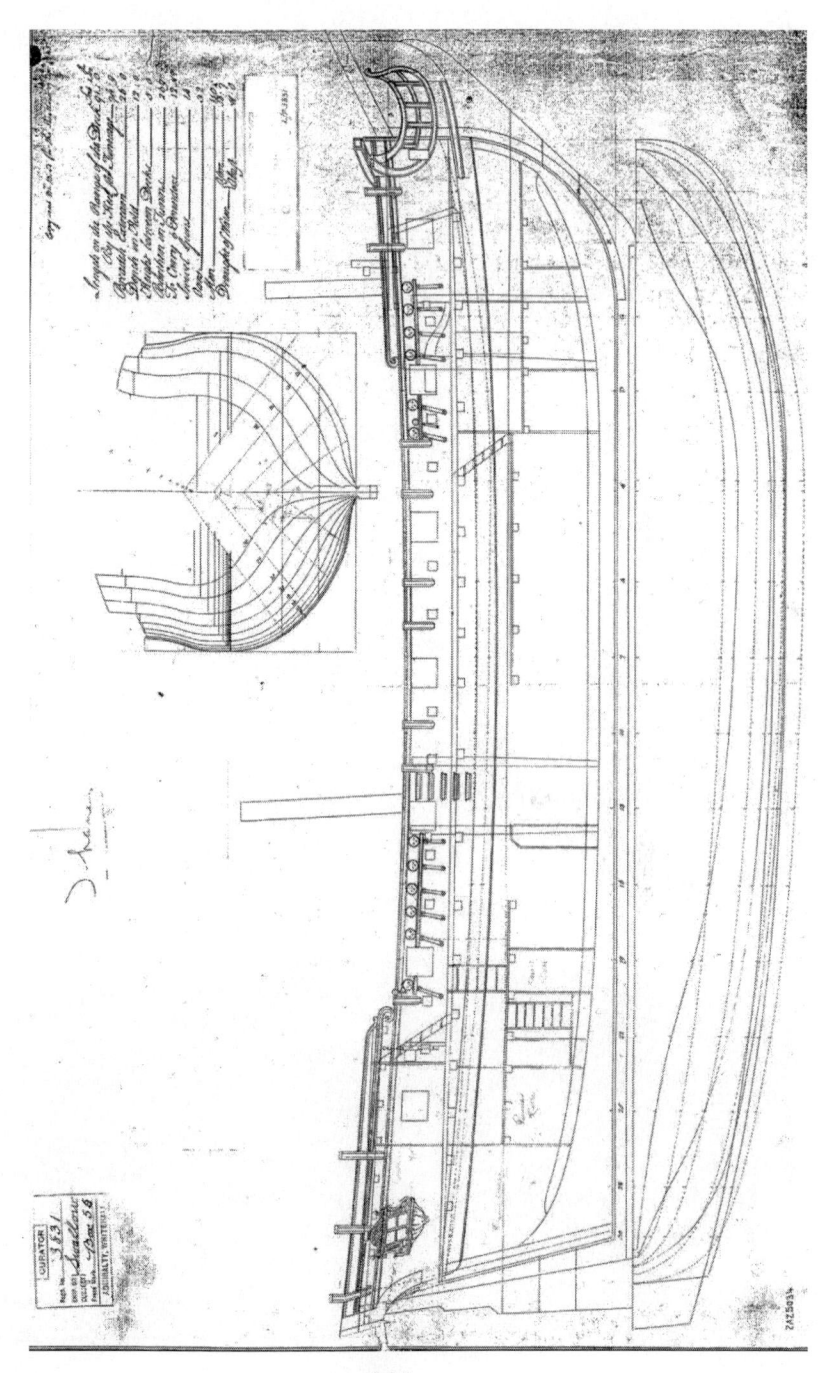

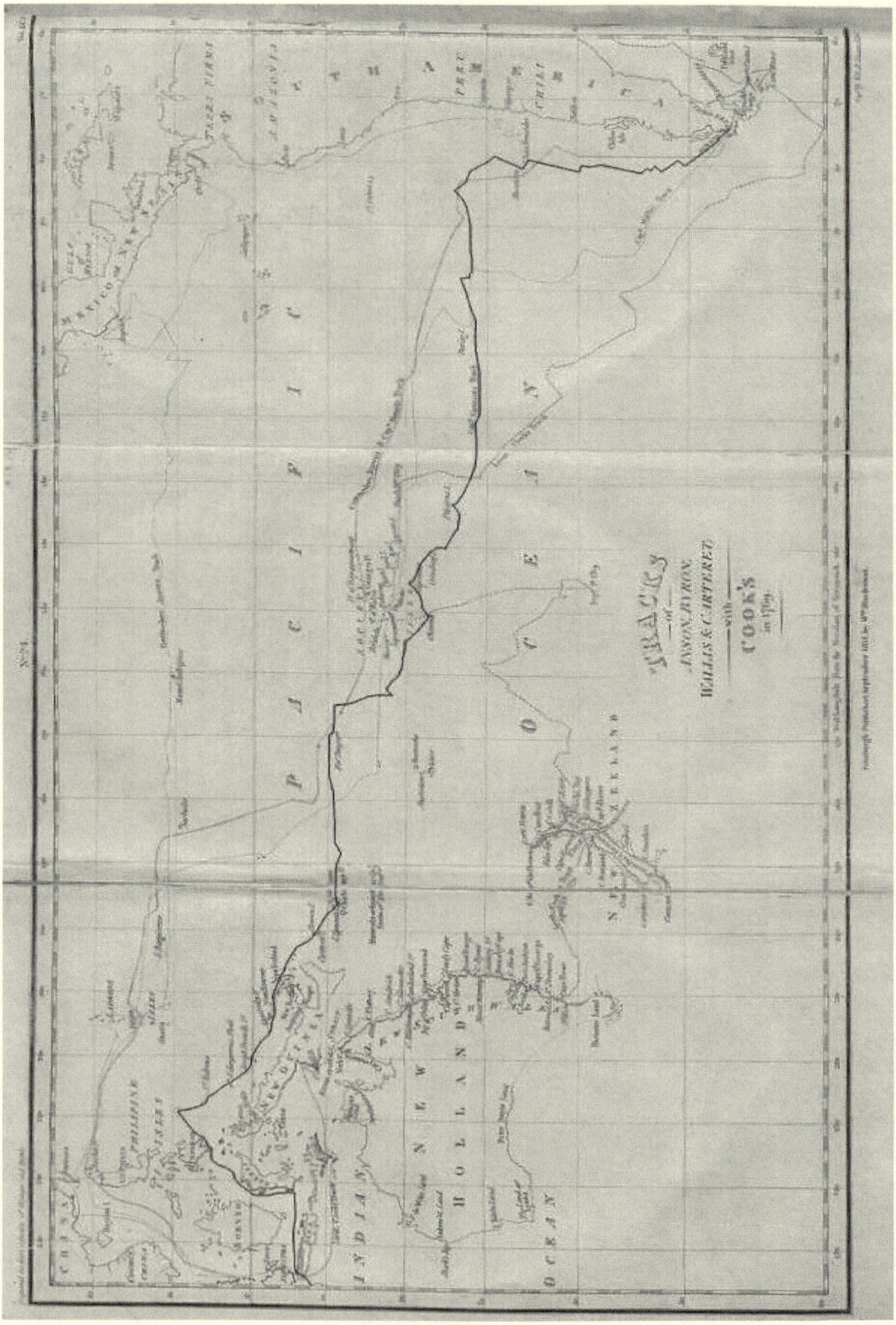

TRACKS
of
ANSON, BYRON,
WALLIS & CARTERET
with
COOK'S
PACIFIC
OCEAN
NEW HOLLAND
NEW ZEALAND
INDIAN OCEAN

Acknowledgements

I would like thank Helen Wallis for permission to use quotes from 'Carteret's Voyage Round the World' and my wife Jeanne for typing and proofreading the manuscript.

References

1. "Carteret's Voyage Round the World, 1766-1769". Edited by Helen Wallis, Cambridge Univesity Press, 1965
2. "Carteret's Voyage round the world, 1766-1769 Volume II". Edited by Helen Wallis, Cambridge Univesity Press, 1965
3. "An Account of the Voyages Undertaken by the Order of His Present Majesty for Making Discoveries in the Southern Hemisphere and Successively Performed by Commodore Byron, Captain Wallis, Captain Carteret, and Captain Cook, in the *Dolphin*, the *Swallow*, and the *Endeavor*, Drawn Up from the Journals Which Were Kept by the Several Commanders, and from the Papers of Joseph Banks, Esq. Hawkesworth, John, Printed for W. Strahan and T. Cadell", 1773
4. Personal Papers of Carteret, Philip, Rear-Admiral, Ca.1733-1796, National Maritime Museum, Greenwich, London
5. A letter from Philip Carteret Esquire, Captain of the *Swallow* Sloop, to Matthew Maty published in Philosophical Transactions (1683-1775) Vol. 60 (1770) pp.20-26, published by the Royal Society.

Index

Admiralty, 3, 4, 6, 7, 8, 11, 12, 13, 14, 22, 23, 29, 30, 31, 33, 37, 39, 41, 42, 64, 67, 89, 121, 156
Ascension, 191
Augusta, 4

Bad Man's Shoal, 131
Batavia, 90, 106, 135, 139, 147, 151, 185
Bay of Disappointment, 23
Beagle, 21, 32
Bishop of Osnabery, 68
Bladort, 180
Boelen, 151
Bonthain, 157
Bonthain Bay, 158
Borneo, 145
Bras, 129
Butulaki, 147
Byron, 3, 4, 8, 14, 33, 38, 41, 70, 74, 77, 79, 91, 120, 151

Cabo Norte, 45
Calcutta, 182
California, 11
Cap Pilar, 21, 26, 28, 31, 32
Cape Froward, 23
Cape Gazelle, 117
Cape Holland, 23, 26
Cape St George, 103
Cape St. Augustin, 135
Cape Town, 185, 190
Cape Trevanion, 92
Cape Verde, 19
Cape Verde Islands, 19
Cape Virgin Mary, 20, 21, 23
Captain Cook, 20, 73, 207
Carteret, 3, 4, 5, 6, 7, 8, 11, 12, 13, 14, 15, 16, 17, 18, 20, 21, 22, 23, 24, 26, 27, 28, 29, 30, 31, 32, 33, 34, 35, 36, 37, 38, 39, 41, 43, 44, 45, 47, 48, 49, 50, 51, 52, 54, 55, 56, 58, 59, 60, 62, 63, 65, 66, 67, 68, 69, 70, 71, 73, 74, 75, 76, 78, 79, 80, 81, 82, 85, 86, 87, 88, 89, 90, 91, 92, 93, 94, 96, 97, 116, 118, 120, 131, 135, 137, 138, 140, 142, 144, 145, 146, 151, 156, 185, 190
Carteret Point, 116
Celebes, 130, 147
Chatham, 3, 12, 15, 16, 36, 37, 60, 76
Chile, 6, 33, 59
Cooper's Island, 180
Cornwall, 8, 14
Crooked Reach, 26
Cumberland Bay, 38, 39

Dampier, 33, 102, 130, 134, 135, 142
Dampier's Bay, 134, 135, 142
Darwin, 21, 22
Davis, 62, 63, 64
De Mathie, 199
Deptford, 14, 126
Desolation Island, 23
Doldrums, 19
Dolphin, 3, 8, 12, 14, 16, 22, 24, 26, 27, 28, 29, 33, 41, 43, 45, 72, 77, 151
Douglas, 151
Drake, 14, 102
Dudley, 181, 183
Duke of York Island, 117, 118
Duroure, 126

Egmont Island, 93, 94, 119, 123
Egmont Isle, 96, 98
Endymion, 199, 200
English, 4
English Cove, 119, 130
English Harbour, 107
Equinox, 124

Falkland Islands, 11, 12, 14, 23, 90
Famedo, 129
Flamborough, 198
Funchal, 15

George Edgecumbe, 3
Gower, 8, 16, 17, 46, 48, 49, 55, 56, 59, 67, 81, 82, 83, 89, 91, 93, 96, 97, 121, 134, 135, 136, 139, 146, 152
Green Island, 102

Harcourt, 182
Holland, 151, 190

Indian Ocean, 185
Islas de Hombres Blanco, 126
Isles of Direction, 33

Jacobus Heere, 149
James Cooper, 100
James Fogarty, 86, 101
Jan Hendrik Voll, 153
Java Head, 188
Jersey, 3
John Fernandes Island, 33
John Hendrik Crouch, 20
Joseph Freewill Islands, 129, 131
Journal, 16, 17, 20, 30, 33, 43, 49, 51, 56, 60, 62, 65, 67, 76, 85, 90, 92, 93, 95, 117, 120, 147, 189

Kar Muaras, 145
Kerton, 32, 33, 35, 38, 45, 48, 51, 53, 57, 59, 60, 63, 65, 66, 69, 71, 74, 78, 79, 82, 84, 87, 91, 95, 104, 118, 123, 131, 143, 152
King George III, 79

La Boudeuse, 193, 194, 195
Le Cerff, 151
Le Maire, 102, 121

Leeward Islands, 12
Levant, 199

Macassar, 144, 147, 154, 157
Macassar Strait, 145
Madeira, 14, 15, 16, 20, 49, 51, 158
Magellan, 20, 41, 102
Mas Afuera, 38, 41, 42, 43, 56, 58, 59, 70, 77, 78, 82
Mas-Afuera, 33
Matty's Island, 126
Medea, 199
Medway, 5, 12, 13
Mew Island, 187
Michael Walker, 126
Millbanke, 4
Mindanao, 130, 134, 135, 143
Monmouth, 4
Mount Pica Ruevo, 15
Mururoa, 68, 69

Navy, 3, 5, 6, 18, 151, 156
New Britain, 93, 99, 117, 118
New Ireland, 117, 118
New Ireland Coast, 118
Nore, 12, 13, 14
Nova Hibernia, 123

Pacific Ocean, 11, 27, 28, 33, 41, 70
Phillip York, 185
Phillipines, 130
Pitcairn, 8, 65, 67, 82, 84, 88
Plymouth, 14, 148
Point Dungeness, 21
Point Siep, 143
Port Famine, 19, 21, 22, 23, 59
Porto Praya, 19
Prince Frederick, 12, 14, 22
Princes Island, 186
Pulo Maratua, 145
Punta Langlois, 42, 45, 50, 51, 52
Punta Negra, 47

Quiros, 69, 73

Ra del Sandalo, 42
Ramos Isle, 97
Renshaw, 6, 72, 86
Roaring Forties, 35
Robert Brown, 94
Robinson Crusoe Island, 33
Roebuck, 114
Royal Reach, 26
Royal William, 201

Salisbury, 3
Sandwich, 199, 200
Santa Cruz Islands, 73
Sarangani Bay, 143
Schouteri, 121
Shabander, 153, 158
Simpson, 8, 20, 21, 28, 29, 42, 52, 59, 79, 80, 81, 82, 83, 84, 85, 86, 87, 89, 91, 93, 97, 118, 125
Simpson Island, 97
Solomon Island, 95
South America, 11, 20
Spain, 3, 39
Spermondes, 147
Spice Islands, 70, 149, 157
St Albans, 4
St Ambrose, 60
St Felix, 60
St George's Bay, 102, 116
St Jago, 19
St Malo, 3
Stephens Islands, 126
Straits of Magellan, 19, 20, 27, 31, 32, 75, 148
Straits of Sunda, 185

Swallow, 3, 4, 5, 6, 7, 8, 9, 11, 12, 13, 14, 19, 20, 21, 22, 23, 24, 26, 27, 28, 29, 30, 31, 32, 33, 34, 35, 36, 37, 38, 39, 41, 42, 43, 44, 45, 46, 47, 48, 49, 50, 51, 52, 53, 54, 55, 56, 57, 58, 59, 60, 61, 62, 63, 64, 65, 66, 67, 68, 69, 70, 71, 72, 73, 74, 75, 76, 77, 78, 79, 80, 81, 82, 84, 85, 86, 87, 88, 89, 90, 91, 92, 93, 94, 96, 97, 116, 118, 119, 123, 131, 135, 137, 138, 139, 142, 144, 146, 151, 156, 185, 190, 192, 207

Tamar, 4
Tamar Island, 27
Tasman, 102
The Mother and Daughters, 116
The Thumb, 148
Thomas Allen, 126
Tinaka Point, 135, 137, 138, 141, 142
Tropic of Cancer, 19, 65

Upright Bay, 26

Vanguard, 4
Viceroy, 15

Wallis, 12, 13, 14, 15, 19, 21, 23, 24, 27, 28, 29, 30, 72, 75, 103
Wallis Island, 104
West Bay, 39
Westminster Hall Island, 28
Wheatly, 153
Wuvulu, 126

Printed in Great Britain
by Amazon.co.uk, Ltd.,
Marston Gate.